I0119165

Robert Howie, Archibald Alexander Hodge, Benjamin Breckinridge
Warfield

Westminster doctrine anent holy scripture

With notes on recent discussions

Robert Howie, Archibald Alexander Hodge, Benjamin Breckinridge Warfield

Westminster doctrine anent holy scripture
With notes on recent discussions

ISBN/EAN: 9783743373570

Manufactured in Europe, USA, Canada, Australia, Japa

Cover: Foto ©Thomas Meinert / pixelio.de

Manufactured and distributed by brebook publishing software
(www.brebook.com)

Robert Howie, Archibald Alexander Hodge, Benjamin Breckinridge
Warfield

Westminster doctrine anent holy scripture

WESTMINSTER DOCTRINE

ANENT

HOLY SCRIPTURE:

TRACTATES BY

PROFESSORS A. A. HODGE AND WARFIELD,

WITH NOTES ON RECENT DISCUSSIONS.

BY

REV. ROBERT HOWIE, M.A.

GLASGOW:

DAVID BRYCE AND SON.
EDINBURGH: R. W. HUNTER.
1891.

PREFATORY NOTE.

THE title I have adopted shows that, while referring to the Proceedings of the Free Church Confession of Faith Committee, my
remarks are confined to the discussions anent Holy Scripture.
If objection be taken to my action in thus divulging what took
place in the Committee regarding this matter, my apology must
be that it is one in respect to which there is much anxiety
throughout the Church. Besides, the leading motions proposed
in the Committee have been already made public, partly by the
authority of the Committee and partly without its authority.
In view of the somewhat misleading accounts of the proceedings of the Committee that have reached the public, and of the
fact that a construction has been put on the finding finally
adopted, different from what would occur to the "plain man,"
and certainly from what was intended by myself and others,
it seems to me absolutely necessary, if further misunderstanding is to be prevented, that a fuller account should be given
to the Church, and especially to members of the ensuing
Assembly, of what took place in the Committee than is em-
bodied in its brief Report.

First Chapter of the Confession. At the same time, in view of anxiety expressed in regard to the Church's position on this subject, the Committee cordially avail themselves of the opportunity of recording their full and steadfast adherence to the doctrines laid down in the Confession as to the great truths of the inspiration, infallible truth, and Divine authority of Holy Scripture as proceeding from God who is the Author thereof. They resolve to bring this finding under the special attention of the General Assembly."

Referring to the foregoing finding *The British Weekly* of March 26, in an article entitled "The Positive Side," says, "The positive truth about inspiration urgently needs to be set forth. Much of the mischief wrought by criticism comes from the negative being presented alone. Thus timid minds are thrown into confusion where nothing seems stable. The Free Church of Scotland Committee at present engaged in revising the Confession have agreed to a very strong statement of their positive views on inspiration, the meaning of which, as the plain man will take it, is to affirm inerrancy. That this is not the real meaning is proved by the fact that many of those who supported the declaration have declared themselves convinced that the absolute accuracy of Scripture on all matters of fact cannot be entertained. While sensible of the difficulty, we are yet strongly of opinion that the Church, in the coming struggle to enlist the new generation under the old banner, will only succeed by absolute candour. This may lose something at first. We see that the ministers in the United States are complaining that their young men's Bible-Classes have been greatly lessened by the publication of Dr. Briggs' manifesto ; but in the end true sincerity and fearlessness will win the day. We have printed this week a sermon by one of the most able and scholarly theologians in Scotland, which presents the subject under some fresh aspects."

In reply, I wrote a letter to the Editor, of which the following are extracts :—" You seem so to misunderstand the real state of things in the Free Church of Scotland as to discredit the good faith of 'many' of those who supported the declaration just issued by the Confession of Faith Committee.

"I am glad that you frankly admit that 'the plain man' will

take 'the very strong statement of their positive views on inspiration' issued by the Committee as meaning 'to affirm
inerrancy.' That undoubtedly is the only legitimate meaning
of the words used, and in that sense they were accepted
by myself and others. 'Error' is surely excluded by an
affirmation of 'infallible truth,' even as it is excluded by
the word 'inspiration' properly understood, and by the words
'as proceeding from God who is the Author thereof.' I cannot
be guilty of the blasphemy of holding that God 'who is Truth
itself' inspired 'error,' or that He is the 'Author' of 'error.'
You say :—'That this [viz., the 'meaning' attached to it by
'the plain man'] is not the real meaning is proved by the
fact that many of those who supported the declaration have
declared themselves convinced that the absolute accuracy
of Scripture on all matters of fact cannot be entertained.'

"I do not know to whom you refer in this connection. What
I do know is that a motion was made in the Committee in the
following terms :—' The Committee, after the fullest inquiry
and discussion, find that it is neither necessary nor expedient
to modify in any way the chapter on Holy Scripture. They
unanimously accept and approve the statements of the Confession on this great subject. They differ, however, as to the
inference to be drawn from the assertion regarding the infallible truth and Divine authority of Holy Scripture. Some
of their number contend that this declaration implies the
absolute freedom from error in every respect of Scripture as
originally given, and say that a statement to this effect should
accompany the Confession. But the Committee cannot accept
this view. The language quoted cannot be regarded as necessarily involving it, and is loyally accepted by many who
refuse to admit the alleged inference. The Committee, in
view of the opinions held on this topic by many eminent and
orthodox divines, and of the discussions on it taking place in
our own and other countries, are of opinion that it would be
in the highest degree unwise for them, or for the Church, to
close a question which the Confession certainly leaves open.
Besides, the known views of the Reformers touching Scripture,
and the principle on which the Westminster Divines proceeded in framing this chapter, make it improbable, in the

judgment of the Committee, that the alleged inference was
held by the Westminster Divines themselves.'

"While a motion was made in these terms by a member of
the Committee, whom you would probably associate with Mr.
Denney as 'one of the most able and scholarly theologians in
Scotland' (all are 'able and scholarly' who take one side on
this question, while those who take the other side are 'uninstructed Evangelicals'), the motion did not find a seconder
as thus expressed. A young lawyer offered to second it, if
sundry amendments which he suggested were made in its
terms. I daresay it will not surprise you that the motion,
both in its original and in its amended form, was vigorously
opposed by such members of the Committee as Messrs. Wallace,
Matthew, Salmond, and myself, who have consistently opposed
the views of Dr. Dods.

"But you will be more surprised when I add that the motion
in question was no less vigorously opposed by Mr. Ross Taylor
(who stated in the Committee that he disapproved of the use
of the terms 'errors' and 'immoralities' as applied to Holy
Scripture. . . . The motion was also opposed by Mr. Robert G.
Balfour and by Dr. Rainy, who left the Chair for the purpose,
and made one of the most satisfactory speeches on the subject
(satisfactory I mean from my point of view) to which I have
ever listened.

"Nor is that all. Even Dr. Blaikie, who, at the previous
meeting of the Committee had read a long paper on the same
lines as the 'Whither?' of Dr. Briggs, and had made the same
quotations from the writings of the Westminster divines, . . .
confessed at the close of the debate that he had got so much
new light in the course of the discussion, that he appealed to
the young theologian who had proposed the motion to with-
draw it. By this time it had been made abundantly manifest
that if that motion had been persisted in, it would have been
rejected by an overwhelming majority of the members of the
Committee who were present. Doubtless coming to the conclusion that in the circumstances, 'discretion was the better
part of valour,' the proposer of the motion asked leave to with-
draw it, and the finding of the Committee, as published, was
declared to be 'unanimous.'

" In view of these facts, I leave you to judge whether you are now entitled to give an interpretation to the finding of the Committee different from what occurs to 'the plain man.' The simple fact is that, living as you do in England, you seem to be grievously misled by some of your correspondents as to the real state of belief on this subject in the Free Church of Scotland. You evidently assume that all who voted in favour of Dr. Dods at last Assembly, and who thus expressed their admiration for the man, also sympathize with his views, and are prepared to endorse all his utterances on the subject of Holy Scripture including the very worst of all (if correctly reported), viz. that contained in the *Christian World* of November 20th, 1890, which simply makes the individual consciousness the supreme arbiter as to what parts of Scripture are to be accepted as true and authoritative.

" So far is this from being the case, I have been assured by large numbers of those who voted in the last Assembly, even for the motion of Mr. Renny, that (now that they better understand the question at issue, as expounded in the pamphlets we have issued, and as formulated in a paper lodged by four of us with the Confession of Faith Committee, for the very purpose of clearing away all irrelevancies) they are entirely at one with us on the doctrinal question. . . . . .

" I have always attached main importance in this matter to the Church's own testimony to the true doctrine of Holy Scripture. That being secured, I have always been prepared to leave not a little to the honour and honesty of those who voluntarily subscribe her creed, but I am sure that 'the plain man' will have little respect for the honour or honesty of the man who endorses such a statement as is made by the Confession of Faith Committee, and yet goes on affirming that there *were* errors in the Scriptures as originally given."

In the *British Weekly* of April 2 an article appeared headed, "Inspiration and 'the Plain Man,'" in which a summary (slightly inaccurate) was given of my letter. The Editor added in the way of reply :—" Some members of the Committee at least must differ from the interpretation of the 'plain man,' or else they have changed their views. We cordially agree with our friend that the churches had better deal honestly with the 'plain man.' He is beginning to look askance, and not without good reason."

I thank the Editor for remarks so opportune. If they apply to any of those who have concurred in the finding of the Confession of Faith Committee, or (what is equivalent) have subscribed the Confession itself (for the finding of the Committee simply reduplicates upon its phraseology), I hope they will be laid to heart. It is high time that it should be understood in clerical circles that the "plain man" is somewhat scandalized, when he finds professed adhesion to the Scriptures or to the Confession followed by attempts to give to their statements a non-natural meaning—a meaning contrary to what occurs to himself.

Better surely even a shorter creed with honest subscription than a professed adherence to our present creed and dishonest subscription.

While saying this, I will not be so uncharitable as to suppose that those who subscribe the Confession and interpret it in a non-natural way are consciously dishonest. They seem always to be able somehow to persuade themselves that their views are really covered by the Confession. The motion in the Confession of Faith Committee above referred to, while professing continued adherence to the Confession, declared that the language of the Confession cannot be regarded as necessarily involving "absolute freedom from error in every respect of Scripture as originally given," and that it is "loyally accepted by many who refuse to admit the alleged inference." Whether by introducing the words "in every respect" the proposer of the motion sought to provide for himself and his friends a way of escape by saying, as some others have done, that there are in Scripture "errors" in grammar, and that the style is not faultless as viewed from their standpoint, I do not know.* But certainly if he understands by "error" what the "plain man" takes it to mean, viz. the logical opposite of truthful statement, I cannot see how the assertion of "infallible truth" (a Confessional phrase homologated by the Committee) can be consistent with holding that there were "errors" in the Scrip-

* See on this point the paper on "Inspiration," by Drs. A. A. Hodge and Warfield, p. 49.

tures as proceeding from " God (who is Truth itself), the Author thereof." It is surely no mere "inference" to say that "infallible truth" excludes "error" as thus defined.

This motion also proposed that the Confession of Faith Committee should declare that it is "improbable" (Dr. Briggs speaks more confidently on the subject) that the "alleged inference was held by the Westminster divines themselves." Such an assertion on the part of a young theologian can scarcely excite surprise, considering the fact referred to by me in my letter to the Editor of *The British Weekly*, viz. that at one of the meetings of the Committee, Dr. Blaikie read a long and elaborate paper on the lines of Dr. Briggs, with the view of proving that the framers of the Confession held that there were "errors" in the Scriptures as originally given. Some of us were wicked enough to suggest that the paper in question should be published, so that the Church might have an opportunity of knowing what is taught her students by one of her senior professors, and that an opportunity might be given of refuting its statements in detail.

Considering that such a paper was read; that similar allegations as to the import of the Confession and the views of its framers are made in the "Whither?" of Dr. Briggs; and that we may yet hear of them on the floor of the Assembly or otherwise (even although they received so little countenance in the Confession of Faith Committee), I have felt it to be my duty to anticipate their possible promulgation by republishing the thoroughly conclusive Reply by Dr. Warfield to Dr. Briggs on " The Westminster Doctrine of Inspiration " (see pp. 64-74).

That reply was first brought under my notice in a letter by Dr. Warfield to myself in which he says:—" With reference to the question you ask, I should say that it ought not to be a very difficult matter to convince open-minded people that the *Westminster Confession* teaches the verbal inspiration and inerrancy of the Scriptures. Men who wish to have it otherwise can close their minds to any proof. The phrases employed, taken together, absolutely require this interpretation: *e.g.* the words in I. viii. '*being immediately* inspired by God' have a definite historical sense, and can be given no other

honestly. Let anybody look into any document of the times—
e.g. Ball's *Catechism*—to see what 'immediately inspired' was
intended to teach.

"I should proceed (1) by bringing together the numerous
phrases bearing on the point in the *Confession ;* and expound-
ing their meaning : (2) by showing that these phrases *historically* mean verbal inspiration and inerrancy and nothing else :
so that a contrary interpretation is reading a new and un-
intended meaning into perfectly explicit words: and (3) by
showing that the framers of the Confession all held the
strictest theory of inspiration and meant to express it in these
words, with which they were wont to express it. I was
amazed to hear Dr. Blaikie speak doubtingly of the old Scotch
doctrine. Surely someone will refute him out of the mouths
of the fathers. Dr. Briggs made a similar statement as to the
Westminster Divines, and I showed in *The Independent* its
absolute incorrectness. The Westminster Divines without exception held to a very strict theory, and it is easy to excerpt
them and prove it."

In another letter, when forwarding his Reply to Dr. Briggs,
and authorizing its republication, Dr. Warfield says :—"I
regret that it is only a fragment of what might be done : but
the limits of a newspaper article are rather narrow for such a
discussion. The truth is that the attempt to foist any other
sense than the strictest on our Confession is the most hopeless
of tasks—if we are to interpret *historically :* and scarcely less
so if we confine ourselves to the limits of the document.
The truth is that our Westminster fathers were inclined to a
mechanical theory of *dictation,* rather than to a *loose* theory.
I hope some one of your collaborateurs will do at least as much
for the Scotch worthies as my little paper does for the Westminster men."

In order to make perfectly intelligible the strictures
appearing in the "Whither ?" of Dr. Briggs, on the views on
inspiration of the Princeton Divines, and, at the same time,
show to what an extent these views have been misrepre-
sented by Dr. Blaikie, in his Letter to Dr. Bonar, I (with the
permission of Dr. Warfield) also republish the Tractate on
"Inspiration" written by Dr. A. A. Hodge and himself. I

do this the rather because I had circulated that Tract among members of the Committee, and was thanked by Mr. (now Dr.) Ross Taylor for having thereby contributed to the clearing away of misconceptions and misunderstandings, and thus aided in bringing about the unanimous finding of the Committee.

In now republishing these valuable papers, I do not wish to stir up the embers of the fires of controversy, but rather to extinguish them by diffusing such instruction and information as will tend to dispel the confusion of thought on this whole question which so widely prevails.

I do this the more willingly because Dr. Blaikie was frank enough to admit at the close of the debate that he had got new light; thus showing the importance of clear exposition. He in particular expressed satisfaction with a statement I had made on the closing night of the debate to the effect that when we speak of the "infallible truth" of Holy Scripture we do not mean that everything recorded in Scripture is in itself true or right. I instanced the sayings of devils and of wicked men, which may be in themselves untrue, but are always truthfully recorded,—to be refuted by God; and I affirmed that, in such cases, the Scriptures are responsible, not for the lies of Satan or of wicked men, but for the Divine refutation thereof. As I had already dealt with the same point in my published Reply to Dr. Blaikie (pp. 17, 18), I was amazed that when giving expression to a truism with which I had supposed every one to be familiar, it should thus have been regarded as an admission that brought great relief to the Professor's mind, and convinced him that after all we were not so far apart as he had at first supposed. My amazement was all the greater, because at an early stage in the discussion four of us had (as I have indicated in my letter to the Editor of *The British Weekly*) lodged a Statement for the purpose of clearing away irrelevancies and preventing misconceptions on the part of our brethren as to the views we held, and so arriving, if possible, at a common understanding. In that paper we had been careful to specify the points we deemed essential, as also those which we were prepared to regard "as within the sphere of reverent criticism, so far as such criticism does not traverse the statements of Scripture or of the Confession."

We made it perfectly clear that, while concerned about the *product* of inspiration—viz. *a book of infallible truth and Divine authority*, we had no desire to commit the Church to any theory as to the *mode* of inspiration. Lest we might seem to ask the Church to commit herself to any theory as to mode, we refrained even from using the word "verbal," employed by Dr. Warfield, although Dr. Blaikie, in 1880, in correction of a statement he had made to me two years before, said:—"I do believe in the doctrine of verbal *inspiration*; what I cannot receive is, the doctrine of verbal *dictation*."

Our statement was as follows:—"Although the Confession makes no reference to human authorship as concerned in the production of Holy Scripture, it assumes that the men through whom the Lord committed to writing the knowledge of His will were used by Him as *men* with their personal idiosyncrasies.

"This Church does not regard her Confession as laying down any theory as to the *mode* of inspiration. As respects the *product* of inspiration, however, she holds, as taught in the Confession, that the Scriptures of the Old and New Testaments are all given by inspiration of God, so that they are 'the Word of God written,' and whoever may have been their human authors, 'God (who is Truth itself) is the Author thereof.'

"While holding that 'the full persuasion and assurance of the infallible truth and Divine authority' of these Scriptures is due to 'the inward work of the Holy Spirit bearing witness by and with the Word in the heart,' this Church, at the same time, holds, and regards her Confession as teaching, that as given by their Divine Author, these Scriptures are, in all their statements of fact, as well as of doctrine and duty, infallibly true and divinely authoritative, irrespective of their reception by individuals.

"While this Church thus holds all the statements of the original Scriptures to be true in the sense divinely intended; that sense being also consistent with a fair use of words within the range of legitimate human speech, this is consistent with her regarding as within the sphere of reverent criticism, so far as such criticism does not traverse the statements of Scripture or of the Confession, all questions relating to—(1) the dates and human authors of particular parts of Scripture; (2) the sources whence these authors derived their information regarding particular facts ; (3) the progressive character of the revelation of God's will both as respects doctrine and duty communicated through them ; (4) the distinction to be drawn between the sayings and doings of men and devils, which may in themselves not be true or right, but are always truthfully recorded, and the use made of these in Scripture ' for doctrine, for reproof, for correction, for instruction in righteousness ' ; (5) the due recognition of the fact that, on the one hand, different accounts of the same transaction may vary in the expression, in the fulness or compression of the report, in the aspects which receive emphasis or prominence, and yet be all alike true ; and that, on the other hand, as regards reports of sayings or discourses, inspiration does not guarantee verbatim reporting more than any other kind of reporting ; (6) the literary characteristics of the Bible ; (7) the correspondence of the present text of Scripture, or of any particular version or translation with the Scriptures as originally given ; (8) the meaning to be attached to particular statements of Scripture.

"While the various readings prove that copyists were not miraculously preserved from mistakes in transcription, and while uncertainty has thus been created in regard to the original text of particular verses or words, this Church holds that no doctrine or duty revealed in the Bible is affected by these various readings, and *in that sense* she explains the declaration made in sect. 8, chap. 1 of her Confession, viz., ' the Old Testament in Hebrew (which was the native language of the people of God of old), and the New Testament in Greek (which at the time of the writing of it was generally known to the nations), being immediately inspired by God, and by His singular care and providence kept pure in all ages, are therefore authentical ; so as in all controversies of religion, the Church is finally to appeal unto them.'

" The Church holds that the apparent inaccuracies in incidental and subordinate matters which have been regarded as difficulties may be accounted for in other ways than by supposing any real inaccuracy to have been in the Scriptures as originally given.

"ROBERT HOWIE.   JOHN M'EWAN.
"ANDREW INGLIS.   GEORGE WALLACE."

When this detailed statement was made on our part, it was met by assurances on the part of brethren who had been prominent in their support of Dr. Dods, to the effect that equally with ourselves they regarded Scripture as infallibly true and divinely authoritative, irrespective of its reception by individuals; and that they disapproved of the use of the terms "errors" and "immoralities" as applied to Scripture. So soon as that was done, it became obvious that, notwithstanding the paper of Dr. Blaikie, which threatened to bring our discussion to an abrupt termination, the great majority of the Committee could not be far apart in their views on the doctrinal questions involved.

That agreement ultimately found expression in a motion of which Dr. Ross Taylor gave notice, which, after sundry amendments, was seconded by myself, and became the unanimous finding of the Committee.

In the debate of last year, on the case of Dr. Dods, I pressed for the appointment of a Committee to confer with him, in the hope that, in view of the assurances of his supporters, we might arrive, if possible, at a common understanding. I then said:— "If, as our brethren assure us, and if, as the motion of Dr. Adam supposes, Dr. Dods is in harmony with the Church as respects her doctrine—if, as it declares, he has given a strong declaration of adherence to the doctrine of the Church—if that is true, then I do not see why we should not try to get into conference with him, and prevent this matter from being agitated throughout the Church in our Church Courts." The Committee then asked was not appointed, and the result has been agitation to a certain extent in our Church Courts and otherwise. But that agitation has been prevented from assuming an acute form by the knowledge that some of us were doing our best, in the first instance, to ascertain by mutual conference in the Confession of Faith Committee, whether there are irreconcilable differences in the Church in regard to the inspiration, infallible truth, and Divine authority of Holy Scripture, the Church's supreme standard.

The main drawback connected with these conferences was the fact that neither Dr. Dods nor Dr. Bruce was present (although the latter was a member of the Committee), and that thus the Church is still left in ignorance as to whether they will concur in the unanimous finding of that Committee, and loyally accept it when endorsed by the Assembly.

If, however, their absence is, in one aspect, to be regretted, in another, it may have contributed to a speedier agreement. The doctrinal question has been happily discussed on its own merits, apart from the bearing of the Committee's finding upon any individual.

May I express the hope, that in a similarly fearless fashion, the Assembly will realize its duty to the Great Head of the Church, in a matter which so largely concerns His honour, and that, in the presence of other churches and of an unbelieving world (sorely in need of such a testimony), it will boldly avow the " full and steadfast adherence of the Church to the doctrines laid down in the Confession as to the great truths of the inspiration, infallible truth, and Divine authority of Holy Scripture as proceeding from God who is the Author thereof."

From numerous communications made to me, and from the large numbers (from every part of the country) who have indicated their adherence to the " Statement " issued by the Committee " on the cases of Drs. Dods and Bruce," I have the best means of knowing that only thus can mutual confidence, peace, and harmony be restored throughout the Church. It is simply impossible for me to convey any adequate conception of the anxiety that exists on this subject, especially among office-bearers and members.

Of the intensity of conviction that exists not a few of our ministers and congregations have had proof in the withdrawal from the Free Church of office-bearers and members (a fact which I greatly deplore); while many others, as I have been assured by themselves, only remain in her fellowship in the hope that a deliverance will be adopted by next Assembly in harmony with the finding of the Confession of Faith Committee.

Ominous rumours have already been put into circulation to

the effect, that although unable to carry their point in the Confession of Faith Committee, and not having the courage to show the comparative insignificance of their following by proceeding to a division, the "forward movement" party (who went the length of proposing in the Committee to treat as an open question what Books should be included in the Canon), may yet propose a deliverance in the Assembly in the line of the motion which was withdrawn, and thus prevent a unanimous finding of the Assembly.

I can scarcely credit such a rumour. But if this is the policy to be pursued, I have no hesitation in saying that peace will be impossible. Nay more, if peace is to be lasting, and if confidence is to be fully restored, there must be more than a deliverance of the Assembly in harmony with the finding of the Confession of Faith Committee. Individual professors and ministers must hereafter loyally respect that deliverance in their teaching and public utterances. If, through the discussions that have taken place, they have not yet got sufficient light to lead them (to use the phrase of *The British Weekly*) to "change their views," they must at least, so long as they continue in the Church, discontinue those "intemperate" utterances, in which, on the one hand, they misrepresent the views of their brethren, and, on the other, convey the impression that they regard it as their main mission to prove that there were "errors" in the Scriptures as originally given, and thus to subvert faith in the Word of God, and seriously to hinder the work of the Christian ministry.

In last Assembly, the late Dr. Adam, referring specially to the theory of Dr. Dods on inspiration, according to which "the sacred writers were not guarded against inaccuracies of all kinds," said that it "involved tremendous risks," and put the pertinent questions: "Here was a principle, and where were they to stop in its application? Here was a chink, and would it not open, would it not widen, until the whole flood came rushing in?"

Already the truth of these words has been verified, and that too notwithstanding the finding of last Assembly, that the Church "views the use of the term 'mistakes and immoralities' to describe recognized difficulties in the Scriptures as utterly unwarranted, and fitted to give grave offence."

The "chink" is opening. Did not Dr. Blaikie, in his Letter to Dr. Bonar, warmly espouse the cause of Dr. Dods? Have there not been other utterances of a similar kind by less influential men? And then as regards Dr. Dods himself. So far from publicly modifying the views condemned by last Assembly; so far from ceasing those "intemperate" utterances on which the College Committee animadverted; so far from yielding to the remonstrances even of some of his supporters, he has, since last Assembly, made statements of such an objectionable and offensive kind, that anyone who may desire to institute proceedings against him, under the re-affirmed Confession of Faith, will not be under the necessity of raising any question as to whether the finding of last Assembly went far enough in condemnation of his views, and of thus dealing with a *res judicata*. On the contrary, he will be able to plead that the fresh utterances of Dr. Dods, since last Assembly, are specially worthy of condemnation, because they are even more sweeping and far-reaching in their consequences than those dealt with by that Assembly, while their promulgation is more blameworthy, in view of the action already taken in his case, first by the Assembly of 1878 and then by that of 1890.

In my Reply to Dr. Blaikie (pp. 41-42), I have dealt with one of these utterances, viz., that contained in *The British Weekly* of October 2, 1890. All now needed in this connection is to give extracts from a letter I received from the Editor of that paper and from my reply to him. He says: "I was not aware I had used the phrase 'uninstructed Evangelicals' which you quote, and I am sorry I did. There are 'uninstructed Evangelicals' just as there are 'uninstructed Broad-Church men,' but such phrases are on the whole both offensive and untrue." To this I replied: "When I quoted the words 'uninstructed Evangelicals,' I did not mean to say that they had been used by yourself, although they appeared in *The British Weekly* . . . The words . . . as you will see from my Reply to Dr. Blaikie (p. 5) were used by Dr. Dods in an article in *The British Weekly* of date October 2, in which he flagrantly misrepresents the opinions of those opposed to him by declaring that they affirm 'That Christianity stands or falls with the absolute inerrancy of every clause of Scripture,' and represents them as combining 'with Secularists, Atheists, and anti-Christians in general to betray the Christian position.' I know of no 'Evangelical in Scotland who affirms 'that Christianity stands or falls with the absolute inerrancy of every clause of Scripture.' Apart from the fact that some clauses in Scripture contain, as I said in my last, the lies of Satan and of wicked men, which are truthfully recorded in order to be refuted, it is surely one thing to contend for the inerrancy of the original Scriptures, properly understood and defined, and quite another thing to make it the foundation of Christianity.* This is a specimen however of the misrepresentations of our views with which we are familiar in this controversy, another being, that we are contending for the theory of mechanical inspiration or verbal dictation. These misrepresentations, though again and again repudiated, seem to be reiterated for the purpose of proving that all 'Evangelicals' who contend for the inerrancy of the original Scriptures are 'uninstructed,' and that they 'combine with Atheists, Secularists, and anti-Christians in general to betray the Christian position' . . . I am glad that you so frankly admit that there are 'uninstructed Broad-Church men' even as there are 'uninstructed Evangelicals,' and that with myself you deprecate the use of such phrases as ' on the whole both offensive and untrue.' "

Another of the "intemperate" utterances of Dr. Dods was very fully reported in *The Christian World* of Nov. 20, 1890. When I directed the attention of the Confession of Faith Committee to what appeared to be its underlying principle, viz. that the individual consciousness is the supreme arbiter of what parts of the Bible are to be accepted as infallibly true and divinely authoritative, there was on the part of all who spoke an emphatic repudiation of such a principle, and an affirmation of the objective truth and authority of the Bible, irrespective of its "finding" the individual. But I was reminded, that as I

---

* See the beliefs of Evangelicals on this point, well stated by Dr. Warfield at pp. 28, 29.

had not put myself into personal communication with Dr. Dods I had no right to assume that the report in question correctly represents what he actually said on the occasion referred to. Some of his friends have even gone the length of telling me in private that they do not believe he could utter such statements as are there imputed to him, and urged in support of that view the self-contradictory character of some of the reported utterances.

No one will rejoice more than myself if Dr. Dods is in a position to say that the report in question is inaccurate, and either point out clearly and definitely in what respects he has been misreported, or publish a correct version of what he actually did say in addressing the students of Edinburgh University.

I humbly submit that, in view of the extraordinary nature of the statements reported to have been uttered by him—their self-contradictory character—the combination of Rationalism, Mysticism, and Romanism they exhibit,—it was clearly the duty of Dr. Dods from a regard both to his own reputation and to that of the Church of which he is a Professor, to have long ere this made the necessary correction, if he has been to any extent misreported, and the more so as attention has been publicly called on more than one occasion to that report.

While I do not admit that all the ministers of the Church are bound to put themselves into personal communication with Dr. Dods before animadverting on statements publicly reported to have been made by him, especially after he has failed to correct the report when his attention has been called to it (as was done in my Reply to Dr. Blaikie, a copy of which was forwarded to Dr. Dods), I am still so unwilling to believe that he could have made the statements in question, that I forbear further comment until he states publicly whether in any respect that report requires correction. I shall content myself with quoting it *verbatim et literatim*—as follows :—

"THE AUTHORITY OF THE BIBLE."

"Professor Marcus Dods lectured on Friday evening to the Edinburgh University Theological Society on 'The Seat of Authority in

Religion.' Protestantism, he remarked in the course of his lecture, is not merely the substitution of one external authority for another—the Church for Scripture—it is rather the exchange of what is outward for what is inward, of what is indirect for what is direct. It is the exchange of God's voice recognized and interpreted by the Church, for God's voice recognized and interpreted by the individual. But he is only half a Protestant who merely transfers his allegiance from the Church to the Bible. To accept the Bible on the Church's authority, and to accept every statement in it as infallibly true, whether it awakes response in the conscience or not, is to remain precisely in the Romanist's position. It is to yield the guidance of our own spiritual affairs to something external to conscience, and thereby separate ourselves from God. The two extreme positions are equally untenable. It is impossible to maintain the infallibility of the Bible on the ground of its literal accuracy ; and it is impossible to maintain that the Bible is not infallible because there may be found in it inaccuracies. That the Bible was not meant to be used as a mechanical standard of truth is proved by the fact that it is not infallible in all its particular statements. Literal and mechanical accuracy in minute details was evidently not aimed at, or, at all events, has not been attained. From the discrepancies we find we cannot but conclude that in the Gospels we do not possess an account of our Lord's words and actions flawlessly accurate in all details. We have reports which vary and sometimes contradict one another, and which cannot both be accurate. Yet there are persons who say they will give up the Bible altogether if there be one proved error in it, that their salvation depends on the absolute accuracy of every word and sentence from the first verse of Genesis to the last of Revelation. Their salvation depends on no such thing. It is the merest infatuation to say it does. Our faith depends on a living Person who cannot be separated from us, and Who drew to Himself and redeemed many before ever there was a written New Testament. The Bible is infallible as a guide to those who, with childlike spirit and seeking the truth, follow its light. It actually leads men to Christ. It is infallible in its substance, though not in its form, as a whole though not in each particular part, in the spirit though not always in the letter.

"The discrepancies, in themselves trifling and of no consequence, become of alarming consequence when used as a lever to subvert the infallibility of Scripture by writers who take advantage of the claim of literal infallibility advanced by well-intentioned persons. This claim is easily disposed of by means of those discrepancies, and the inference is drawn that the infallibility for which we contend does not exist. But literal infallibility is not that for which we contend, and those discrepancies might be multiplied a hundredfold and yet not be inconsistent with true infallibility.

" For, first, unimportant errors in detail are never allowed to discredit a historian. The rule '*Falsus in uno, falsus in omnibus*' is followed in the case of a deliberate falsifier, but is absurd if applied to one who errs through lack of knowledge. One who intentionally deceives you, a witness on oath who deliberately gives false witness, cannot any more be trusted, and the whole of his evidence is discredited; but there is no man who would not occasionally stumble into error—error at once condoned, and which casts no shadow on his general reputation for truth. There is no historian who has not been proved in error; but occasional, unintentional, unimportant error is lost to view in the general reputation for accuracy which the historian acquires. But what is unimportant error? Is not all error important where Divine and eternal interests are concerned? No! else God would have provided for the absence of all error. Error is unimportant when it does not affect the purpose of the whole. No errors in Scripture are important which do not hinder it from conveying to us an adequate apprehension of God's revelation. It must be judged by its fulfilment of its object, which was to enable us to apprehend God in Christ, and lead us to Him. To deny that it has fulfilled this object is too audacious even for scepticism. The Christian ages stand behind us loudly witnessing that Scripture has done its work. Here we find the 'impregnable rock' of Scripture. No Church or criticism can come in between my soul and the Figure it presents. That Figure I see in the Gospels I find also in my life. The same patience and wisdom and divinity that command my adoration in the Gospels shine on my life and give it all the worth and hope it has. Criticism may cut off a fringe or a tassel from His garments, but the features and expression it cannot touch. They shine with self-evidencing power into every perplexed heart.

" It is feared by some that if we frankly accept the Reformation principle it will leave every man to be the judge of what is Scripture and what is not, and that even when a book is acknowledged to be apostolic it remains with the individual to say how much of it he is pleased to receive as God's Word. But this is practically our present method of treating the Bible. Who is at the reader's elbow as he reads Exodus and Leviticus to tell him what is of *permanent* authority and what was for the Mosaic dispensation alone? Who whispers as we read Genesis and Kings, 'This is exemplary ; this is not'? Who sifts for us the speeches of Job and enables us to treasure as divine truth what he utters in one verse while we reject the next as Satanic ravings? Who gives the preacher accuracy,— who gives him authority of aim to pounce on a sound text in Ecclesiastes while wisdom and folly toss and roll over one another in confusion and inextricable contortions? What enables the humblest Christian to come safely through all the cursing Psalms and go straight to forgive his enemy? What tells us we may eat things strangled though the whole college of apostles deliberately and expressly prohibit such eating? Who assures us we need not anoint the sick with oil though James bids us do so? In a word, how is it that the simplest reader can be trusted with the Bible, and can be left to find his own spiritual nourishment in it? Paul solves the whole matter for us in his bold and exhaustive words, 'The spiritual man—the man who has the Spirit of Christ—judgeth all things.' This, and only this, is the true touchstone by which all things are tried. Let a man accept Christ and His Spirit, and there is no fear of him rejecting what Christ means he should receive.

"Two things effectually prevent an extreme individualism. First, the Christian knows that certain men were commissioned and equipped by Christ to teach His religion, who therefore come with enormous *primâ facie* evidence in their favour. Towards their writings, whose truth has been verified by thousands of every generation finding in them the God and Saviour their souls craved, no reverence can be too great. Second, the extremest Christian individualist must acknowledge the Church of which he is but a small member. If there be lessons which do not find him, and elicit cordial response in him, he remembers that he is not the whole Church for whom Scripture is needed ; and that what seems to him useless may be to another full of help; and that, as his own experience varies, what he considers a stone to-day he may find to be the bread of life at some future period."

As showing further how unsatisfactory are the public utterances of another of our professors, and how impossible it is for a co-presbyter to draw from him any definite statement of his positive beliefs in regard to important truths which he seems to have controverted or ignored, I have, for the information of the Church, now published (pp. 81-86), letters sent by me to Professor Drummond with reference to his *Pax Vobiscum*. They sufficiently explain why his letters in reply are not included. As the Professor excludes reporters from his meetings with students, so, when I wrote to him in regard to his published booklet, and intimated at the outset that my letters to him might be published, he insisted on marking his replies as "private."

I have also reprinted (pp. 75-80), critiques by Dr. Warfield which appeared in the April number of the New York *Presbyterian and Reformed Review*; an Extract from the Writings of the late Principal Cunningham; and the leading article of the *King's Own* for February last. I do so the rather, because they embody in the smallest possible compass the essential principles involved in this controversy.

In republishing in Scotland these valuable papers, written by men held in high esteem in all Presbyterian, and, indeed, in all Evangelical Churches, it is my aim to make Confessional truth so plain that there shall be no further ground of offence. Very specially do I desire that there shall be no misunderstanding in regard to so vital a point as the Church's doctrine of Holy Scripture—a point which must be settled and sure, if there is to be any agreement whatever on other Scripture doctrines.

In conclusion, let me say that I regret exceedingly that in this controversy, now drawing to a close, as I hope, I have come into renewed collision with professors for whom I have a high personal regard, and from whose published writings I have derived not a little profit. My present references to their utterances since last Assembly are made most reluctantly, but made under a solemn sense of duty, and in the earnest hope that these professors may yet volunteer public explanations of so satisfactory a kind in regard to the matters to which I have thus directed attention, as to allay anxiety throughout the Church and restore confidence in their teaching.

"Shall the sword devour for ever?" Are not the ordinary ministers of the Church (who are brought face to face with the baneful effects of uncertainty as to Divine verities) entitled to ask that their efforts to commend the Word of God, the God of the Word, and the Saviour therein revealed, shall not be counteracted by the "intemperate" and mischievous utterances of those occupying influential positions in the Church, and entrusted with the training of her future ministers?

In presence of the remarkable fact that the Scriptures, of whose inspiration, infallible truth, and Divine authority the other proofs are so abundant, have during recent years been receiving from archæological discoveries fresh confirmation, even in their most minute details,* we may surely expect our theologians of "light and leading" soon to cease their rash, irreverent, unproved, and unprovable assertions as to the existence of errors in these Scriptures, as they proceeded from "God (who is Truth itself) the Author thereof," especially as such assertions contradict the express testimony of Scripture and of our Lord and His Apostles.

---

* (See pp. 50-54). Canon Tristram says :—"Looking back for less than forty years, it requires no small effort to grasp the vast advance which has been made in a single generation in the confirmation and illustration of Old Testament history from external sources. The sepulchres of Egypt have been ransacked, the mounds of Assyria and Babylonia have been excavated, the hills and rivers of Palestine have been searched, and the result is that there is scarcely a single incident, wherever the sacred narrative impinges on the history or transactions of neighbouring nations, in which the minute accuracy of the Biblical record is not established."

TRACTATE ON INSPIRATION.

BY

PROFESSOR ARCHIBALD A. HODGE, D.D., LL.D.,

AND

PROFESSOR BENJAMIN B. WARFIELD, D.D.

(Reprinted, by permission.)

THE word " Inspiration," as applied to the Holy Scriptures, has gradually acquired a specific technical meaning independent of its etymology. At first this word, in the sense of " God-breathed," was used to express the entire agency of God in producing that divine element which distinguishes Scripture from all other writings. It was used in a sense comprehensive of supernatural revelation, while the immense range of providential and gracious divine activities concerning the genesis of the word of God in human language was practically overlooked. But Christian scholars have come to see that this divine element, which penetrates and glorifies Scripture at every point, has entered and become incorporated with it in very various ways, natural, supernatural and gracious, through long courses of providential leading, as well as by direct suggestion—through the spontaneous action of the souls of the sacred writers, as well as by controlling influence from without. It is important that distinguishable ideas should be connoted by distinct terms, and that the terms themselves should be fixed in a definite sense. Thus we have come to distinguish sharply between Revelation, which is the frequent, and Inspiration, which is the constant, attribute of all the thoughts and statements of Scripture, and between the problem of the genesis of Scripture on the one hand, which includes historic processes and the concurrence of natural and supernatural forces, and must account for all the phenomena of Scripture, and the mere fact of inspiration on the other hand, or the superintendence by God of the writers in the entire process of their writing, which accounts for nothing whatever but the absolute infallibility of the record in which the revelation, once generated, appears in the original autograph. It will be observed that we intentionally avoid applying to this inspiration the predicate "influence." It summoned, on occasion, a great variety of influences, but its essence was superintendence. This superintendence attended the entire process of the genesis of Scripture, and particularly the process of the final composition of the record. It interfered with no spontaneous natural agencies, which were, in themselves, producing results conformable to the mind of the Holy Spirit. On occasion it summoned all needed divine influences and suggestions, and it sealed the entire record and all its elements, however generated, with the imprimatur of God, sending it to us as his Word.

The importance of limiting the word "inspiration" to a definite and never-varying sense, and one which is shown, by the facts of the case, to be applicable equally to every part of Scripture, is self-evident, and is emphasized by the embarrassment which is continually recurring in the discussions of this subject, arising sometimes from the wide, and sometimes from the various, senses in which this term is used by different parties. The history of theology is full of parallel instances, in which terms of the highest import have come to be accepted in a more fixed and narrow sense than they bore at first either in scriptural or early ecclesiastical usage, and with only a remote relation to their etymology; as, for instance, Regeneration, Sacrament, etc.

PRESUPPOSITIONS.

From this definition of the term it is evident that instead of being, in the order of thought, the first religious truth which we embrace, upon which, subsequently, the entire fabric of true religion rests, it is the last and crowning attribute of those sacred books from which we derive our religious knowledge. Very many religious and historical truths must be established before we come to the question of inspiration: as, for instance, the being and moral government of God, the fallen condition of man, the fact of a redemptive scheme, the general historical truth of the Scriptures, and the validity and authority of the revelation of God's will, which they contain— *i.e.* the general truth of Christianity and its doctrines. Hence it follows that, while the inspiration of the Scriptures is true, and, being true, is a principle fundamental to the adequate interpretation of Scripture, it nevertheless is not in the first instance a principle fundamental to the truth of the Christian religion. In dealing with sceptics it is not proper to begin with the evidence which immediately establishes inspiration, but we should first establish theism, then the historical credibility of the Scriptures, and then the divine origin of Christianity. Nor should we ever allow it to be believed that the truth of Christianity depends upon any doctrine of inspiration whatever. Revelation came in large part before the record of it, and the Christian Church before the New Testament Scriptures. Inspiration can have no meaning if Christianity is not true, but Christianity would be true and divine—and, being so, would stand—even if God had not been pleased to give us, in addition to his revelation of saving truth, an infallible record of that revelation absolutely errorless by means of inspiration.

In the second place, it is also evident that our conception of revelation and its methods must be conditioned upon our general views of God's relation to the world, and his methods of influencing the souls of men. The only really dangerous opposition to the Church doctrine of inspiration comes either directly or indirectly, but always ultimately, from some false view of God's relation to the world, of his methods of working, and of the possibility of a supernatural agency penetrating and altering the course of a natural process. But the whole genius of Christianity, all of its essential and most characteristic doctrines, presuppose the immanence of God in all his creatures, and his concurrence with them in all of their spontaneous activities. In him, as an active, intelligent Spirit, we all live and move and have our being. He governs all his creatures and all their actions, working in men even to will and spontaneously to do his good pleasure. The currents, thus, of the divine activities do not only flow around us, conditioning or controlling our action from without, but they none the less flow within the inner current of our personal lives, confluent with our spontaneous self-movements, and contributing to the effects whatever properties God may see fit that they shall have.

There is also a real logical and ideal, if not a physical, continuity between all the various provinces and methods of God's working : providence and grace, the natural and the supernatural, all constitute one system in the execution of one plan. All these agents and all these methods are so perfectly adjusted in the plan of God that not one interferes with any other, and all are so adjusted and controlled as that each works perfectly, according to the law of its own nature, and yet all together infallibly bring about the result God designs. In this case that design is a record without error of the facts and doctrines he had commissioned his servants to teach.

Of the manner in which God may inform and direct a free intelligence without violating its laws we have a familiar analogy in Nature in the relation of instinct to free intelligence. Intelligence is personal, and involves self-consciousness and liberty. Instinct is impersonal, unconscious, and not free. Both exist alike in man, with whom intelligence predominates, and in the higher animals, with whom instinct predominates. In every case the instinct of the creature is the intelligence of the Creator working through the creature's spontaneity, informing and directing, yet never violating any of the laws of his free intelligence. And in Nature we can trace this all the way from the instinct of the bee, which works mechanically, to the magic play of the æsthetic instincts, which largely constitute the genius of a great artist. We are not absurdly attempting to draw a parallel between natural instinct and supernatural inspiration. But the illustration is good simply to show that as a matter of fact God does prompt from within the spontaneous activities of his intelligent creatures, leading them by unerring means to ends imperfectly discerned by themselves ; and that this activity of God, as in instinct or otherwise, does not in any wise reveal itself, either in consciousness or in the character of the action to which it prompts, as interfering with the personal attributes or the free rational activities of the creature.

THE GENESIS OF SCRIPTURE.

We allude here to this wide and as yet imperfectly explored subject only for the purpose of distinctly setting apart the various problems it presents, and isolating the specific point of inspiration, with which we, as well as the Church in general, are more particularly interested. All parties of believers admit that this genesis of Holy Scripture was the result of the co-operation, in various ways, of the agency of men and the agency of God.

The human agency, both in the histories out of which the Scriptures sprang, and in their immediate composition and inscription, is everywhere apparent, and gives substance and form to the entire collection of writings. It is not merely in the matter of verbal expression or literary composition that the personal idiosyncrasies of each author are freely manifested by the untrammelled play of all his faculties, but the very substance of what they write is evidently for the most part the product of their own mental and spiritual activities. This is true except in that comparatively small element of the whole body of sacred writing in which the human authors simply report the word of God objectively communicated, or, as in some of the prophecies, they wrote by divine dictation. As the general characteristic of all their work, each writer was put to that special part of the general work for which he alone was adapted by his original endowments, education, special information and providential position. Each drew from the stores of his own original information, from the contributions of other men and from all other natural sources. Each sought knowledge, like all other authors, from the use of his own natural faculties of thought and feeling, of intuition and of logical inference, of memory and imagination, and of religious experience. Each gave evidence of his own special limitations of knowledge and mental power, and of his personal defects as well as of his powers. Each wrote upon a definite occasion, under special historically grouped circumstances, from his own standpoint in the progressively unfolded plan of redemption, and each made his own special contribution to the fabric of God's word.

The divine agency, although originating in a different source, yet emerges into the effect very much through the same channels. The Scriptures have been generated, as the plan of redemption has been evolved, through an historic process. From the beginning God has dealt with man in the concrete, by self-manifestations and transactions. The revelation proceeds from facts to ideas, and has been gradually unfolded as the preparation for the execution of the work of redemption has advanced through its successive stages. The general providence unfolding this plan has always been divine, yet has also been largely natural in its method, while specially directed to its ends, and at the same time surcharged along portions of its line, especially at the beginning and at great crises, with the supernatural, as a cloud is surcharged with electricity. There were divine voices, appearances, covenants, supernatural communications and interventions—the introduction of new institutions, and their growth under special providential conditions. The prophet of God was sent with special revelations and authority at particular junctures to gather and interpret the lessons of the past, and to add to them lessons springing out of the providential conditions of the present. The Scriptures were generated through sixteen centuries of this divinely-regulated concurrence of God and man, of the natural and the supernatural, of reason and revelation, of providence and grace. They are an organism consisting of many parts, each adjusted to all the rest, as the "many members" to the "one body." Each sacred writer was by God specially formed, endowed, educated, providentially conditioned, and then supplied with knowledge naturally, supernaturally or spiritually conveyed, so that he, and he alone, could, and freely would, produce his allotted part. Thus God predetermined all the matter and form of the several books largely by the formation and training of the several authors, as an organist determines the character of his music as much when he builds his organ and when he tunes his pipes as when he plays his keys. Each writer also is put providentially at the very point of view in the general progress of revelation to which his part assigns him. He inherits all the contributions of the past. He is brought into place and set to work at definite providential junctures, the occasion affording him object and motive, giving form to the writing God appoints him to execute.

The Bible, moreover, being a work of the Spirit for spiritual ends, each writer was prepared precisely for his part in the work by the personal dealings of the Holy Spirit with his soul. Spiritual illumination is very different from either revelation or inspiration, and yet it had, under the providence of God, a large share in the genesis of Scripture, contributing to it a portion of that divine element which makes it the word of God. The Psalms are divinely-inspired records of the religious experience of their writers, and are by God himself authoritatively set forth as typical and exemplary for all men for ever. Paul and John and Peter largely drew upon the resources and followed the lines of their own personal religious experience in the intuitional or the logical development of their doctrine; and their experience had, of course, been previously divinely determined for that very purpose. And in determining their religious experience God so far forth determined their contributions to Scripture. And he furnished each of the sacred writers, in addition to that which came to him through natural channels, all the knowledge needed for his appointed task, either by vision, suggestion, dictation or elevation of faculty, or otherwise, according to his will. The natural knowledge came from all sources, as traditions, documents, testimonies, personal observations and recollections—by means also of intuitions, logical processes of thought, feeling, experience, etc.; and yet all were alike under the general direction of God's providence. The supernatural knowledge became confluent with the natural in a manner which violated no law of reason or of freedom. And throughout the whole of his work the Holy Spirit was present, causing his energies to flow into the spontaneous exercises of the writer's faculties, elevating and directing where need be, and everywhere securing the errorless expression in language of the thought designed by God. This last element is what we call "Inspiration."

In all this process, except in a small element of prophecy,

c

34

it is evident that as the sacred writers were free and active in
their thinking and in the expression of their thoughts, so they
were conscious of what they were doing, of what their words
meant, and of the design of their utterance. Yet, even then,
it is no less evident that they all, like other free instruments
of Providence, " builded better than they knew." The mean-
ings of their words, the bearing of the principles they taught,
of the facts they narrated, and the relation of their own part
to the great organism of divine revelation, while luminous
to their own consciousness, yet reached out into infinitely
wider horizons than those penetrated by any thought of
theirs.

STATEMENT OF THE DOCTRINE.

During the entire history of Christian theology the word
" Inspiration " has been used to express either some or all of
the activities of God co-operating with its human authors in
the genesis of Holy Scripture. We prefer to use it in the
single sense of God's continued work of superintendence, by
which, his providential, gracious and supernatural contributions
having been presupposed, he presided over the sacred writers
in their entire work of writing, with the design and effect of
rendering that writing an errorless record of the matters he
designed them to communicate, and hence constituting the
entire volume in all its parts the word of God to us.

While we have restricted the word " Inspiration " to a
narrower sphere than that in which it has been used by many
in the past, nevertheless we are certain that the above statement of the divine origin and infallibility of Scripture accurately expresses the faith of the Christian Church from the
first. Still, several points remain to be more particularly considered, concerning which some difference of opinion at present
prevails.

First. Is it proper to call this inspiration "plenary"? This
word, which has often been made the occasion of strife, is in
itself indefinite, and its use contributes nothing either to the
precision or the emphasis of the definition. The word means
simply " full," " complete," perfectly adequate for the attain-
ment of the end designed. whatever that might have been.

There ought not to be on any side any hesitancy to affirm this of the books of the Bible.

Second. Can this inspiration be properly said to be "verbal"? The objection to the application of this predicate to inspiration is urged upon three distinct grounds:

(1.) We believe that the great majority of those who object to the affirmation that inspiration is verbal are impelled thereto by a feeling, more or less definite, that the phrase implies that inspiration is, in its essence, a process of verbal dictation, or that, at least in some way, the revelation of the thought or the inspiration of the writer was by means of the control which God exercised over his words. And there is the more excuse for this misapprehension because of the extremely mechanical conceptions of inspiration maintained by many former advocates of the use of this term "verbal." This view, however, we repudiate as earnestly as any of those who object to the language in question. At the present time the advocates of the strictest doctrine of inspiration in insisting that it is verbal do not mean that in any way the thoughts were inspired by means of the words, but simply that the divine superintendence, which we call inspiration, extended to the verbal expression of the thoughts of the sacred writers, as well as to the thoughts themselves, and that hence the Bible, considered as a record, an utterance in words of a divine revelation, is the word of God to us. Hence, in all the affirmations of Scripture of every kind there is no more error in the words of the original autographs than in the thoughts they were chosen to express. The thoughts and words are both alike human, and therefore subject to human limitations, but the divine superintendence and guarantee extend to the one as much as the other.

(2.) There are others who, while insisting as strongly as any upon the presence of the divine element in Scripture, developed through special providences and gracious dealings, religious experiences and mental processes, in the very manner we have just set forth under the head of the "Genesis of Scripture," yet substantially deny what we have here called "inspiration." They retain the word "inspiration," but signify by it the divine element in the revelation, or providential or gracious dealing aforesaid, and they believe that the sacred writers, having been divinely helped to certain knowledge, were left to the natural limitations and fallibility incidental to their human and personal characters, alike in their thinking out their several narrations and expositions of divine truth, and in their reduction of them to writing. This view gives up the whole matter of the immediate divine authorship of the Bible as the word of God, and its infallibility and authority as a rule of faith and practice. We have only the several versions of God's revelations as rendered mentally and verbally, more or less adequately, yet always imperfectly, by the different sacred writers. This class of objectors are, of course, self-consistent in rejecting verbal inspiration in any sense. But this view is not consistent either with the claims of Scripture, the consciousness of Christians or the historic doctrine of the Church.

(3.) There are others who maintain that the Scriptures have been certainly inspired so far forth as to constitute them in all their parts, and as a whole, an infallible and divinely-authoritative rule of faith and practice, and yet hold that, while the thoughts of the sacred writers concerning doctrine and duty were inspired and errorless, their language was of purely human suggestion, and more or less accurate. The question as to whether the elements of Scripture relating to the course of Nature and to the events of history are without error will be considered below: it is sufficient to say under the present head that it is self-evident that, just as far as the thoughts of Scripture relating to any element or topic whatsoever are inspired, the words in which those thoughts are expressed must be inspired also. Every element of Scripture, whether doctrine or history, of which God has guaranteed the infallibility, must be infallible in its verbal expression. No matter how in other respects generated, the Scriptures are a product of human thought, and every process of human thought involves language. "The slightest consideration will show that words are as essential to intellectual processes as they are to mutual intercourse. . . . Thoughts are wedded to words as necessarily as soul to body. Without it the mysteries unveiled before the eyes of the seer would be confused shadows; with it, they are made clear lessons for human life." *

Besides this, the Scriptures are a *record* of divine revelations, and as such consist of words; and as far as the record is inspired at all, and as far as it is in any element infallible, its inspiration must reach to its words. Infallible thought must be definite thought, and definite thought implies words.] ut if God could have rendered the thoughts of the apostles regarding doctrine and duty infallibly correct without words, and then left them to convey it to us in their own language, we should be left to precisely that amount of certainty for the foundation of our faith as is guaranteed by the natural competency of the human authors, and neither more nor less. There would be no divine guarantee whatever. The human medium would everywhere interpose its fallibility between God and us. Besides, most believers admit that some of the prophetical parts of Scripture were verbally dictated. It was, moreover, promised that the apostles should speak as the Spirit gave them utterance. "The word of God came unto the prophet." The Church has always held, as expressed by the Helvetic Confession, II., "that the canonical Scriptures *are the word of God.*" Paul claims that the Holy Spirit superintended and guaranteed his words as well as his thoughts (1 Cor. ii. 13). The things of the Spirit we teach "not in the words which man's wisdom teacheth, but which the Holy Ghost teacheth" (συγκρίνοντες), comparing spiritual things with spiritual—*i.e.* spiritual thoughts with spiritual words.

It is evident, therefore, that it is not clearness of thought which inclines any of the advocates of a real inspiration of the Holy Scriptures to deny that it extends to the words. Whatever discrepancies or other human limitations may attach to the sacred record, *the line* (of inspired or not inspired, of infallible or fallible) *can never rationally be drawn between the thoughts and the words of Scripture.*

Third. It is asked again: In what way, and to what extent, is the doctrine of inspiration dependent upon the supposed results of modern criticism as to the dates, authors, sources and

* Canon Westcott's *Introduction to the Study of the Gospels*, 5th edition : Introduction, pp. 14, 15.

modes of composition of the several books? To us the following answer appears to be well founded, and to set the limits within which the Church doctrine of inspiration is in equilibrium with the results of modern criticism fairly and certainly :

The doctrine of inspiration, in its essence—and, consequently, in all its forms—presupposes a supernatural revelation and a supernatural providential guidance entering into and determining the genesis of Scripture from the beginning. Every naturalistic theory, therefore, of the evolution of Scripture, however disguised, is necessarily opposed to any true version of the catholic doctrine of inspiration. It is also a well-known matter of fact that Christ himself is the ultimate witness on whose testimony the Scriptures, as well as their doctrinal contents, rest. We receive the Old Testament just as Christ handed it to us, and on his authority. And we receive as belonging to the New Testament all, and only those, books which an apostolically-instructed age testifies to have been produced by the apostles or their companions—i.e. by the men whom Christ commissioned, and to whom he promised infallibility in teaching. It is evident, therefore, that every supposed conclusion of critical investigation which denies the apostolic origin of a New Testament book or the truth of any part of Christ's testimony in relation to the Old Testament and its contents, or which is inconsistent with the absolute truthfulness of any affirmation of any book so authenticated, must be inconsistent with the true doctrine of inspiration. On the other hand, the defenders of the strictest doctrine of inspiration should cheerfully acknowledge that theories as to the authors, dates, sources and modes of composition of the several books which are not plainly inconsistent with the testimony of Christ or His apostles as to the Old Testament, or with the apostolic origin of the books of the New Testament, or with the absolute truthfulness of any of the affirmations of these books so authenticated, cannot in the least invalidate the evidence or pervert the meaning of the historical doctrine of inspiration.

Fourth. The real point at issue between the more strict and the more lax views of inspiration maintained by believing scholars remains to be stated. It is claimed, and admitted equally on both sides, that the great design and effect of inspiration is to render the Sacred Scriptures in all their parts a divinely infallible and authoritative rule of faith and practice, and hence that in all their elements of thought and expression, concerned in the great purpose of conveying to men a revelation of spiritual doctrine or duty, the Scriptures are absolutely infallible. But if this be so, it is argued by the more liberal school of Christian scholars that this admitted fact is not inconsistent with other facts which they claim are matters of their personal observation : to wit, that in certain elements of Scripture which are purely incidental to their great end of teaching spiritual truth, such as history, natural history, ethnology, archæology, geography, natural science and philosophy, they, like all the best human writings of their age, are, while for the most part reliable, yet limited by inaccuracies and discrepancies. While this is maintained, it is generally at the same time affirmed that when compared with other books of the same antiquity these inaccuracies and discrepancies of the Bible are inconsiderable in number, and always of secondary importance, in no degree invalidating the great attribute of Scripture—its absolute infallibility and its divine authority as a rule of faith and practice.

The writers of this article are sincerely convinced of the perfect soundness of the great catholic doctrine of biblical inspiration—*i.e.* that the Scriptures not only contain, but ARE, THE WORD OF GOD, and hence that all their elements and all their affirmations are absolutely errorless, and binding the faith and obedience of men. Nevertheless, we admit that the question between ourselves and the advocates of the view just stated is one of fact, to be decided only by an exhaustive and impartial examination of all the sources of evidence—*i.e.* the claims and the phenomena of the Scriptures themselves. There will undoubtedly be found upon the surface many apparent affirmations presumably inconsistent with the present teachings of science, with facts of history or with other statements of the sacred books themselves. Such apparent inconsistencies and collisions with other sources of information are to be expected in imperfect copies of ancient writings, from the fact that the original reading may have been lost, or that we may fail to realize the point of view of the author, or that we are destitute of the circumstantial knowledge which would fill up and harmonize the record. Besides, the human forms of knowledge by which the critics test the accuracy of Scripture are themselves subject to error. In view of all the facts known to us, we affirm that a candid inspection of all the ascertained phenomena of the original text of Scripture will leave unmodified the ancient faith of the Church. In all their real affirmations these books are without error.

It must be remembered that it is not claimed that the Scriptures, any more than their authors, are omniscient. The information they convey is in the forms of human thought, and limited on all sides. They were not designed to teach philosophy, science or human history as such. They were not designed to furnish an infallible system of speculative theology. They are written in human languages, whose words, inflections, constructions and idioms bear everywhere indelible traces of human error. The record itself furnishes evidence that the writers were in large measure dependent for their knowledge upon sources and methods in themselves fallible, and that their personal knowledge and judgments were in many matters hesitating and defective, or even wrong. Nevertheless, the historical faith of the Church has always been that all the affirmations of Scripture of all kinds, whether of spiritual doctrine or duty, or of physical or historical fact, or of psychological or philosophical principle, are without any error when the *ipsissima verba* of the original autographs are ascertained and interpreted in their natural and intended sense. There is a vast difference between exactness of statement, which includes an exhaustive rendering of details, an absolute literalness, which the Scriptures never profess, and accuracy, on the other hand, which secures a correct statement of facts or principles intended to be affirmed. It is this accuracy, and this alone, as distinct from exactness, which the Church doctrine maintains of every affirmation in the original text of Scripture without exception. Every statement accurately corresponds to truth just as far forth as affirmed.

PROOF OF THE DOCTRINE.

We of course do not propose to exhibit this evidence in this article. We wish merely to refresh the memory of our readers with respect to its copiousness, variety and cogency.

First. The New Testament writers continually assert of the Scriptures of the Old Testament, and of the several books which constitute it, that they ARE THE WORD OF GOD. What their writers said God said. Christ sent out the apostles with the promise of the Holy Ghost, and declared that in hearing them men would hear him. The apostles themselves claimed to speak as the prophets of God, and with plenary authority in his name binding all consciences. And while they did so God endorsed their teaching *and their claims* with signs and wonders and divers miracles. These claims are a universal and inseparable characteristic of every part of Scripture.

Second. Although composed by different human authors on various subjects and occasions, under all possible varieties of providential conditions, in two languages, through sixteen centuries of time, yet they evidently constitute one system, all their parts minutely correlated, the whole unfolding a single purpose, and thus giving indubitable evidence of the controlling presence of a divine intelligence from first to last.

Third. It is true that the Scriptures were not designed to teach philosophy, science or ethnology, or human history as such, and therefore they are not to be studied primarily as sources of information on these subjects. Yet all these elements are unavoidably incidentally involved in the statements of Scripture. Many of these, because of defective knowledge or interpretation upon our part, present points of apparent confusion or error. Yet the outstanding fact is, that the general conformableness of the sacred books to modern knowledge in all these departments is purely miraculous. If these books, which originated in an obscure province of the ancient world, be compared with the most enlightened cosmogonies or philosophies or histories of the same or immediately subsequent centuries, their comparative freedom even from apparent error is amazing. Who prevented the sacred writers from falling into the wholesale and radical mistakes which were necessarily incidental to their position as mere men? The fact that at this date scientists of the rank of Faraday and Henry, of Dana, of Guyot and Dawson, maintain that there is no real conflict between the really ascertained facts of science and the first two chapters of Genesis, rightly interpreted, of itself demonstrates that a supernatural intelligence must have directed the writing of those chapters. This, of course, proves that the scientific element of Scripture, as well as the doctrinal, was within the scope of inspiration. And this argument is every day acquiring greater force from the results of the critical study of Scripture, and from advanced knowledge in every department of history and science, which continually tend to solve difficulties and to lessen the number of apparent discrepancies.

Fourth. The moral and spiritual character of the revelation which the Scriptures convey of God, of the person of Christ, of the plan of redemption and of the law of absolute righteousness, and the power which the very words of the record, as well as the truths they express, have exercised over the noblest men and over nations and races for centuries,—this is the characteristic self-demonstration of the word of God, and has sufficed to maintain the unabated catholicity of the strict doctrine of inspiration through all change of time and in spite of all opposition.

Fifth. This doctrine of the inspiration of Scripture, in all its elements and parts, has always been the doctrine of the Church. Dr. Westcott has proved this by a copious catena of quotations from Ante-Nicene Fathers in Appendix B to his *Introduction to the Study of the Gospels.* He quotes Clemens Romanus as saying that the Scriptures are "the true utterances of the Holy Ghost." He quotes Tertullian as saying that these books are "the writings and the words of God," and Cyprian as saying that the "gospel cannot stand in part and fall in part," and Clement of Alexandria to the effect that the foundations of our faith "we have received from God through the Scriptures," of which not one tittle shall pass away without being accomplished, "for the mouth of the Lord the Holy Spirit spake it." Dr. Westcott quotes Origen as teaching that the Scriptures are without error, since "they were accurately written by the co-operation of the Holy Ghost," and that the words of Paul are the words of God.

The Roman Church (Can. Conc. Trid., Sess. IV.) says, "God is the author of both" Testaments. The second Helvetic Confession represents the whole Protestant Reformation in saying (Ch. I.): "The canonical Scriptures are the true word of God," for "God continues to speak to us through the Holy Scriptures." The Westminster Confession says: "It pleased the Lord at sundry times and in divers manners to reveal himself and to declare his will unto his Church, and afterward . . . to commit the same wholly unto writing." It declares that the Scriptures are in such a sense given by inspiration, that they possess a divine authority, and that "God is their author," and they "are the WORD OF GOD."

It is not questionable that the great historic churches have held these creed definitions in the sense of affirming the errorless infallibility of the Word. This is everywhere shown by the way in which all the great bodies of Protestant theologians have handled Scripture in their commentaries, systems of theology, catechisms and sermons. And this has always been preeminently characteristic of epochs and agents of reformation and revival. All the great world-moving men, as Luther, Calvin, Knox, Wesley, Whitefield and Chalmers, and proportionately those most like them, have so handled the divine Word. Even if the more lax doctrine has the suffrage of many scholars, or even if it be true, it is nevertheless certain that hitherto in nineteen centuries it has never been held by men who also possessed the secret of using the word of God like a hammer or like a fire.

LEGITIMATE PRESUMPTIONS.

In testing this question by a critical investigation of the phenomena of Scripture, it is evident that the stricter view, which denies the existence of errors, discrepancies or inaccurate statements in Scripture, has the presumption in its favour, and that the *onus probandi* rests upon the advocates of the other view. The latter may fairly be required to furnish positive and conclusive evidence in each alleged instance of error until the presumption has been turned over to the other side. The *primâ facie* evidence of the claims of Scripture is assuredly all in favour of an errorless infallibility of all scriptural affirmations. This has been from the first the general faith of the historical Church and of the Bible-loving, spiritual people of God. The very letter of the Word has been proved from ancient times to be a tremendous power in human life.

It is a question also of infinite importance. If the new views are untrue, they threaten not only to shake the confidence of men in the Scriptures, but the very Scriptures themselves as an objective ground of faith. We have seen that the Holy Spirit has, as a matter of fact, preserved the sacred writers to a degree unparalleled elsewhere in literature from error in the departments of philosophy and science. Who then shall determine the limit of that preserving influence? We have seen that in God's plan doctrine grows out of history, and that redemption itself was wrought out in human history. If, then, the inspiration of the sacred writers did not embrace the department of history, or only of sacred and not of profane history, who shall set the limit and define what is of the essence of faith and what the uncertain accident? It would assuredly appear that, as no organism can be stronger than its weakest part, if error be found in any one element or in any class of statements, certainty as to any portion could rise no higher than belongs to that exercise of human reason to which it will be left to discriminate the infallible from the fallible.

The critical investigation must be made, and we must abide by the result when it is unquestionably reached. But surely it must be carried on with infinite humility and teachableness, and with prayer for the constant guidance of the gracious Spirit. The signs of success will never be presumption, an evident sense of intellectual superiority, or a want of sympathy with the spiritual Church of all ages or with the painful confusion of God's humble people of the present.

With these presumptions and in this spirit let it (1) be proved that each alleged discrepant statement certainly occurred in the original autograph of the sacred book in which it is said to be found. (2) Let it be proved that the interpretation which occasions the apparent discrepancy is the one which the passage was evidently intended to bear. It is not sufficient to show a difficulty, which may spring out of our defective knowledge of the circumstances. The true meaning must be definitely and certainly ascertained, and then shown to be irreconcilable with other known truth. (3) Let it be proved that the true sense of some part of the original autograph is directly and necessarily inconsistent with some certainly-known fact of history or truth of science, or some other statement of Scripture certainly ascertained and interpreted. We believe that it can be shown that this has never yet been successfully done in the case of one single alleged instance of error in the WORD OF GOD.

CRITICAL OBJECTIONS TRIED.

It remains only to consider more in detail some of the special objections which have been put forward against this doctrine in the name of criticism. It cannot be, indeed, demanded that every one urged should be examined and met, but it may be justly expected that the chief classes of relevant objections should be briefly touched upon. This, fortunately, is no illimitable task. There are, as already stated, two main presuppositions lying at the base of the doctrine, essential to its integrity, while to them it adds one essential supposition. The presuppositions are—1. The possibility of supernatural interference, and the actual occurrence of that interference in the origin of our Bible; and, 2. The authenticity, genuineness and historical credibility of the records included in our Bible. The added supposition is—3. The truth to fact of every statement in the Scriptures. No objection from the side of criticism is relevant unless it traverses some one of these three points. The traditional view of the age and authorship of a document or of the meaning of a statement may be traversed, and yet no conflict arise with the doctrine of a strict inspiration. But criticism cannot reach results inconsistent with the genuineness and authenticity of a document judged according to the professions of that document or the state-

ments or implications of any other part of Scripture, or in-
compatible with the truth of any passage in the sense of that
passage arrived at by the correct application of the sound
principles of historico-grammatical exegesis, without thereby
arraying herself in direct opposition to the Church doctrine
of inspiration. All objections to that doctrine based on such
asserted results of criticism are undoubtedly relevant. Our duty
is, therefore, to ask what results of criticism are claimed
which traverse some one of the three assertions—of a supernatural origin for the Scriptures, of genuineness and authenticity for its books, and of absolute freedom from error of its
statements.

I. THE AUTHENTICITY AND INTEGRITY OF THE BOOKS OF THE
OLD AND NEW TESTAMENTS, AS THEY HAVE COME DOWN
TO US.

The first point for us to examine would naturally be the
bearing upon the Church doctrine of inspiration of the various
modern critical theories concerning the origin and present
integrity of the several books of the Old and New Testaments.
This is at present the most momentous question which agitates
the believing world. The critical examination of all the most
intimate phenomena of the text of Scripture is an obvious
duty, and its results, when humility, docility and spiritual
insight are added to competent learning and broad intelligence,
must be eminently beneficial. It is obvious, however, that
this department of the subject could not be adequately discussed in this paper. It is consequently postponed to the near
future, when it is intended that the whole subject shall be presented as fully as possible.

In the mean time, the present writers, while they admit
freely that the traditional belief as to the dates and origin of
the several books may be brought into question without involving any doubt as to their inspiration, yet confidently affirm
that any theories of the origin or authorship of any book of
either Testament which ascribe to them a purely naturalistic
genesis, or dates or authors inconsistent with either their own
natural claims or the assertions of other Scripture, are plainly

inconsistent with the doctrine of inspiration taught by the Church. Nor have they any embarrassment in the face of these theories, seeing that they believe them to rest on no better basis than an over-acute criticism overreaching itself and building on fancies. Here they must content themselves with reference to the various critical discussions of these theories which have poured from the press for detailed refutation of them. With this refutation in mind they simply assert their conviction that none of the claims or assertions of the Scriptures as to the authenticity of a single book of either Testament has hitherto been disproved.

II.—DETAILED ACCURACY OF STATEMENT.

We are next confronted with objections meant to traverse the third of our preliminary statements, consisting of bold assertions that, whatever may have been their origin, our Scriptures do exhibit phenomena of inaccuracy, that mistakes are found in them, errors committed by them, untrue statements ventured. Nor is this charge put forward only by opponents of revelation: a Van Oosterzee, as well as "a Tholuck, a Neander, a Lange, a Stier," admits "errors and inaccuracies in matters of subordinate importance." * It is plain, however, that if the Scriptures do fail in truth in their statements of whatever kind, the doctrine of inspiration which has been defended in this paper cannot stand. But so long as the principles of historico-grammatical exegesis are relied on to determine the meaning of Scripture, it is impossible to escape the fact that the Bible claims to be thus inspired. And thus it is not a rare thing to find the very theologians who themselves cannot believe in a strict inspiration yet admitting that the Scripture writers believed in it.† We cannot, therefore,

---

* See Van Oosterzee's *Dogmatics*, p. 205.

† Thus Tholuck : " Yet his [the author of Hebrews] application of the Old Testament rests on the strictest view of inspiration, since passages where God is not the speaker are cited as words of God or of the Holy Ghost (i. 6, 7, 8 ; iv. 4, 7 ; vii. 21 ; iii. 7 ; x. 15)."—*Old Testament in the New, in Bibliotheca Sacra*, xi. p. 612. So also Richard Rothe : " It is clear, then, that the orthodox theory [*i.e.* the very strictest] of inspiration is countenanced by the authors of the New Testament." So also Canon

occupy the ground on which these great and worthy men seem to us so precariously to stand. A proved error in Scripture contradicts not only our doctrine, but the Scripture claims, and therefore its inspiration in making those claims. It is therefore of vital importance to ask, Can phenomena of error and untruth be pointed out?

There is certainly no dearth of "instances" confidently put forward. But it is abundantly plain that the vast majority of them are irrelevant. We must begin any discussion of them, therefore, by reasserting certain simple propositions, the result of which will be to clear the ground of all irrelevant objections. It is to be remembered, then, that—1. We do not assert that the common text, but only that the original autographic text, was inspired. No "error" can be asserted, therefore, which cannot be proved to have been aboriginal in the text.   2. We do not deny an everywhere-present human element in the Scriptures. No mark of the effect of this human element, therefore—in style of thought or wording—can be urged against inspiration unless it can be shown to result in untruth. 3. We do not erect inspiration into an end, but hold it to be simply a means to an end—viz. the accurate conveyance of truth. No objection, therefore, is valid against the form in which the truth is expressed, so long as it is admitted that that form conveys the truth.   4. We do not suppose that inspiration made a writer false to his professed purpose, but rather that it kept him infallibly true to it. No objection is valid, therefore, which overlooks the prime question: What was the professed or implied purpose of the writer in making this statement? These few simple and very obvious remarks set aside the vast majority of the customary objections. The first throws out of court numbers of inaccuracies in the Old and New Testaments as either certainly or probably not parts of the original text, and therefore not fit evidence in the case. The second performs the same service for a still greater number, which amount simply to the discovery of individual traits, modes of thought

Farrar: "He [Paul] shared, doubtless, in the views of the later Jewish schools— the Tanaim and Amoraim—on the nature of inspiration. These views . . . made the words of Scripture co-extensive and identical with the words of God."—*Life of Paul*, ii. p. 47.

or expression, or forms of argumentation in the writings of the several authors of the biblical books. The third sets aside a vast multitude, drawn from pressure of language, misreading of figures, resurrection of the primary sense of idioms, etc., in utter forgetfulness of the fact that no one claims that inspiration secured the use of good Greek in Attic severity of taste, free from the exaggerations and looseness of current speech, but only that it secured the accurate expression of truth, even (if you will) through the medium of the worst Greek a fisherman of Galilee could write and the most startling figures of speech a peasant could invent. Exegesis must be historical as well as grammatical, and must always seek the meaning *intended*, not any meaning that can be tortured out of a passage. The fourth in like manner destroys the force of every objection which is tacitly founded on the idea that partial and incomplete statements cannot be inspired, no documents can be quoted except *verbatim*, no conversations reported unless at length, etc., and which thus denies the right of another to speak to the present purpose only, appeal to the sense, not wording of a document, give abstracts of discourses, and apply, by a true exegesis, the words of a previous writer to the present need. The sum of the whole matter is simply this: No phenomenon can be validly urged against verbal inspiration which, found out of Scripture, would not be a valid argument against the truth of the writing. Inspiration securing no more than this—*truth*, simple truth—no phenomenon can be urged against verbal inspiration which cannot be proved to involve *an indisputable error*.

It is not to be denied that such phenomena are asserted to be discoverable in the Scriptures. Is the assertion capable of being supported by facts? That is the only question now before us. And it thus becomes our duty to examine some samples of the chief classes of facts usually appealed to. These samples —which will, moreover, all be chosen from the New Testament, and all at the suggestion of opponents—must serve our present needs.

HISTORICAL AND GEOGRAPHICAL ACCURACY.

1. It is asserted that the Scripture writers are inaccurate in their statements of historical and geographical facts, as exhibited by the divergence existing between their statements and the information we derive from other sources, such as profane writers and monuments. When we ask for the proofs of this assertion, however, they are found to be very difficult to produce. A generation or two ago this was not so much the case; but the progress of our knowledge of the times and the geography of the region in which our sacred books were written has been gradually wiping out the " proofs " one by one, until they are at this day non-existent. The chief (and almost the only) historical errors still asserted to exist in the New Testament are—the " fifteenth year of Tiberius " of Luke iii. 1 ; the enrolment during Cyrenius's · governorship of Luke ii. 2 ; and the revolt of Theudas of Acts v. 36. It is not denied that these statements present difficulties, but it is humbly suggested that that is hardly synonymous with saying that they are proved mistakes. *If* Herod died in the spring of A.U.C. 750 (which seems well-nigh certain), and *if*, in Luke iii. 23, the " about " be deemed not broad enough to cover two years (which is fairly probable), and *if* Luke iii. 1 means to date John's first appearance (as again seems probable), and *if* no more than six months intervened between John's and Jesus' public appearance (which, still again, seems probable),—then it is admitted that the " fifteenth year of Tiberius " must be a mistake—*provided that, still further*, we must count his years from the beginning of his sole reign, and not from his co-regnancy with Augustus ; in favour of which latter mode of counting much has been, and more can be, urged. Surely this is not a very clear case of indubitable error, with its *five ifs* staring us in the face. Again, *if* the Theudas mentioned in Acts is necessarily the same as the Theudas mentioned by Josephus, then Luke and Josephus do seem to be in disaccord as to the time of his revolt; and *if* Josephus can be shown to be, in general, a more accurate historian than Luke, then his account must be preferred. But neither of these *ifs* is true. Josephus is the less accurate historian, as is easily proved ; and

there are good reasons—convincing to a critic like Winer and
a Jew like Jost, neither certainly affected by apologetical bias
—to suppose that Acts and Josephus mention different revolts.
Where, then, is the contradiction ?

The greatest reliance is, however, placed on the third case
adduced—the statement of Luke that Jesus was born at the
time of a world-enrolment which was carried out in Syria
during the governorship of Cyrenius. Weiss * offers three
reasons why Luke is certainly incorrect here, which Schurer †
increases to five facts—viz.; 1. History knows nothing of a
general empire-census in the time of Augustus; 2. A Roman
census would not force Joseph to go to Bethlehem, nor Mary to
go with him; 3. Nor could it have taken place in Palestine
in the time of Herod; 4. Josephus knows nothing of such a
census, but, on the contrary, speaks of that of Acts v. 37 as
something new and unheard of; and 5. Quirinius was not
governor of Syria during Herod's life. This has a formidable
look, but each detail has been more than fully met. Thus,
Objection 1 turns wholly upon an *argumentum e silentio*, always
precarious enough, and here quadruply so, seeing that (1) an
empire-census is just such a thing as Roman historians would
be likely to omit all mention of, just as Spatian fails to mention in his life of Hadrian the famous rescript of that monarch,
and all contemporary history is silent as to Augustus's geo-
metrical survey ; (2) We have no detailed contemporary history of this time, the inaccurate and gossiping Suetonius and
Josephus being our only sources of information ; (3) Certain
oft-quoted passages in Tacitus and Suetonius acquaint us with
facts which absolutely require such a census at their base ; and
(4) We have direct, though not contemporary, historical proof
that such a census was taken, in statements of Cassiodorus and
Suidas. Objection 2 gains all its apparent force from a *confusio
verborum*. Luke does not represent this as a Roman census in
the sense that it was taken up after Roman methods, but only
in the sense that it was ordered ultimately by Roman authority.
Nor does he represent Mary as being forced to go to Bethlehem
with Joseph ; her own choice, doubtless, determined her journey.

* Meyer's *Markus und Lukas*, p. 286 (ed. 6).
† *N. T. Zeitgeschichte*, pp. 268-286.

The same *confusio verborum* follows us into Objection 3. It may be improbable that Herod should have been so far set aside that a census should have been taken up in his dominions after Roman methods and by Roman officials; but is it so improbable that he should be ordered to take himself a census after his own methods and by his own officials? Josephus can give us the answer.[*] Whatever may have been Herod's official title, whether *rex socius* or, as seems more probable (one stage lower), *rex amicus Cæsaris*, it is certain that he felt bound to bow to the emperor's every whisper; so that if Augustus desired statistics as to the *regna* (and Tacitus proves he did), Herod would be forced to furnish them for his *regnum*. Objection 4 again is easily laid: Josephus not only mentions nothing he could escape which exhibited Jewish subjection, but actually passes over the decade 750-760 so slightly that he can hardly be said to have left us a history of that time. That he speaks of the later census of Acts v. 37 as something new is most natural, seeing that it was, as carried on by the Roman officials and after Roman methods, not only absolutely new, and a most important event in itself, but, moreover, was fraught with such historical consequences that it could not be passed over in silence. Objection 5 is the most important and difficult, but not, therefore, insuperable. It states, indeed, a truth: Quirinius was not governor of Syria until after Herod's death. But it must be noted, on the one hand, that Zumpt has proved, almost, if not quite, to demonstration, that Quirinius was twice governor of Syria, the first time beginning within six months after Herod's death; and, on the other, that Luke does not say that Christ was born while Cyrenius was governor of Syria. What Luke says is, that Christ was born during the progress of a census, and then defines the census as the first which was carried on when Cyrenius was governor of Syria. If this census was begun under Varus and finished under Quirinius, Christ may have been born, according to Luke, at any time during the progress of this census. This, because Luke ii. 2 is not given to define the time of Christ's birth, but more narrowly to describe what census it was which had in verse 1 been used

[*] Cf. *Ant.*, xv. 10, 4 ; xvi. 2, 5 ; 4, 1 ; 9, 3 ; xvii. 2, 1 ; 2, 4 ; 5, 8 ; 11, 4, etc., for Herod's status.

to define the time of Christ's birth,* Thus, doubtless, it is true that Christ was born under Varus, and yet during the course of the first Quirinian census; and thus Schürer's fifth objection goes the way of all the others.

The wonderful accuracy of the New Testament writers in all, even the minute and incidental, details of their historical notices cannot, however, be made even faintly apparent by a simple answering of objections. Some sort of glance over the field as a whole is necessary to any appreciation of it. There occur in the New Testament some thirty names—emperors, members of the family of Herod, high priests, rabbis, Roman governors, princes, Jewish leaders—some mention of which might be looked for in contemporary history or on contemporary monuments.† All but two of these—and they the insignificant Jewish rebels Theudas and Barabbas—are actually mentioned; and the New Testament notices are found, on comparison, to be absolutely accurate in every, even the most minute, detail. Every one of their statements has not, indeed, passed without challenge, but challenge has always meant triumphant vindication. Some examples of what is here meant have been given already; others may be added in a note for their instructiveness.‡ Now, the period of which

* Take an example : If one should say of any event, that it occurred during our war with Great Britain, and then add, " I mean that war wherein Jackson fought," would he necessarily refer to an event *late* in the war, after Jackson came to the front ? Not so, because *the war alone* defines the time of the event, and Jackson only *which* war. So in Luke the *census alone* defines the time of Christ's birth, and Quirinius only *which* census. It ought to be added that there are at least three other methods of explaining Luke's words, all possible, and none very improbable, on the supposition of any one of which conflict with history is impossible.

† These are: Augustus, Tiberius, Claudius—Herod Antipas, the two Philips, Archelaus, Agrippa I., Agrippa II., Herodias, Herodias' daughter, Bernice, Drusilla—Annas, Caiaphas, Ananias—Gamaliel—Quirinius, Pilate, Felix, Festus, Gallio, Sergius Paulus—Aretas (Candace), Lysanias—[Theudas], Judas of Galilee [Barabbas]. Candace seems to represent a hereditary title, not a personal name ; Theudas and Barabbas are not named in profane sources. Cf. the (incomplete) list and fine remarks of Rawlinson (*Hist. Evidences*, Boston, 1873, p. 195 *sq.*).

‡ It was long boldly asserted that Luke was in error in making Lysanias a contemporary tetrarch with the Herodian rulers. But it is now admitted that Josephus mentions an earlier and a later Lysanias, and so corroborates Luke ; and inscriptions also have been brought forward which supervindicate Luke's accuracy, so that even M. Renan

these writers treat is absolutely the most difficult historical
period in which to be accurate that the world has ever seen.
Nothing was fixed or stable; vacillation, change, was everywhere. The province which was senatorial to-day was im-
perial to-morrow—the boundaries that were fixed to-day were
altered to-morrow. That these writers were thus accurate in a
period and land wherein Tacitus failed to attain complete
accuracy means much.

We reach the same conclusion if we ask after their
geographical accuracy. In no single case have they slipped
here, either; and what this means may be estimated by noting
what a mass of geographical detail has been given us.*
Between forty and fifty names of countries can be counted
in the New Testament pages; every one is accurately named
and placed. About the same number of foreign cities are
named, and all equally accurately. Still more to the purpose,
thirty-six Syrian and Palestinian towns are named, the great
majority of which have been identified,† and wherever testing
is possible the most minute accuracy emerges. Whether due
to inspiration or not, this unvarying accuracy of statement is
certainly consistent with the strictest doctrine of inspiration.

admits it. Again, it was long contended that Luke had inaccurately
assigned a proconsul to Cyprus; but this was soon set aside by a reference to Cyprian coins of Claudius's time and to Dion Cassius, liv. 4; and
now Mr. Cesnola publishes an inscription which mentions the veritable
proconsul Paulus whom Luke mentioned (*Cyprus*, p. 425). So with reference to the titles of the rulers of Achaia, Philippi, Ephesus, etc. (See in
general Lee on *Inspiration*, p. 364, note 2.)

* Compare the efforts of a real forger with the accuracy of these
autoptic writers—*e.g.* of Prochorus, as given in Zahn's *Acta Joannis*, p. lii.
Only nine real places can be found in a long list of geographical names
invented for the need. Thus, to the little Patmos a number of cities and
villages is ascribed which would require a Sicily or Cyprus to furnish
ground to stand on.

† These names are: *Ænon, *Antipatris, †Arimathea, *Azotus, *Beth-
any, †Bethany beyond Jordan, *Bethlehem, ‖Bethphage, §Bethsaida,
§Cana, §Capernaum, *Cæsarea, *Cæsarea Philippi, *Chorazin, 'Dal-
manutha, *Damascus, ‡Emmaus, *Ephraim, *Gadara, *Gaza, §Gerasa,
*Jericho, *Jerusalem, *Joppa, †Jouda, †Kerioth, *Lydda, *Magdala,
*Nain, *Nazareth, *Salim, *Seleucia, *Sychar, *Tiberias, *Tyre. Those
marked * are pretty certainly identified; those †, with great probability;
those §, with a choice between the two places; and those ‖, as to their
neighbourhood. There are, besides, some names quoted from the Old
Testament—*e.g.* Gomorrah, *Rama, *Sarepta, *Shechem, †Sodom. Also
some other geographical names—*e.g.* *The brook Kedron, *Jordan, *the
Mount of Olives, and *the Sea of Galilee, etc.

2. Another favourite charge made against these writers is, that they are often hopelessly inconsistent with one another in their statements; and this charge of disharmony has sometimes been pushed so far as to make it do duty even against their historical credibility. But when we begin to examine the instances brought forward in support of it, they are found to be cases of *difficult*, not of *impossible*, harmony. And it is abundantly plain that it must be shown to be *impossible* to harmonize any two statements on any natural supposition before they can be asserted to be inconsistent. This is a recognized principle of historical investigation, and it is the only reasonable principle possible, unless we are prepared to assert that the two statements necessarily contain all the facts of the case and exclude the possibility of the harmonizing supposition. Having our eyes upon this principle, it is not rash to declare that no disharmony has ever been proved between any two statements of the New Testament. The best examples to illustrate the character of the attempts made to exhibit disharmony, and the rocks on which these attempts always break, are probably those five striking cases on which Dr. Fisher most wisely rests his charge against the complete harmony of the four evangelists—viz. the alleged disharmony in the accounts of the place and phraseology of the Sermon on the Mount, the healing of the centurion's son, the denials of Peter, the healing of the blind man at Jericho, and the time of the institution of the Lord's Supper.* But that in each of these most natural means of harmonizing exist, and are even in some instances recognized as possible by Dr. Fisher himself, President Bartlett has lately so fully shown in detail† that we cannot bring ourselves to repeat here the oft-told tale. Take one or two other examples : for instance, look at that famous case alleged in the specification of the *hour* in John xix. 14 and Mark xv. 25. The difficulty here, says Dean Alford, is insuperable, and with him Meyer *et al.* agree. But even Strauss admits that it would be cancelled "if it were possible

---

* *Beginnings of Christianity,* p. 460 *sq.*
† *Princeton Review,* January, 1880, p. 47 *sq.*

56

to prove that the Fourth Gospel proceeds upon another mode
of reckoning time than that used by the Synoptics." And
that it is possible to prove this very thing any one can satisfy
himself by noting the four places where John mentions the
hour (i. 39 ; iv. 6, 52 ; xix. 14); whence it emerges that John
reckons his hours according to the method prevalent in Asia
Minor*—from midnight, and not from daybreak. Thus all
difficulty vanishes.† The disharmony claimed to exist between
Matt. xxvii. 6-8 and Acts i. 18, 19 is also voided by a naïve
kind of admission ; Dean Alford, for instance, asserting in one
breath that no reconciliation can be found consistent with
common honesty, and in the next admitting that the natural
supposition by which the passages are harmonized is "of course
possible." This admission, on the recognized principles of historical criticism, amounts simply to a confession that no disharmony ought to be asserted in the case.

Perhaps, however, the two most important and far-reaching
instances of disharmony alleged of late years are—that asserted
between the narratives of the events preceding, accompanying
and following the birth of our Lord given by Matthew and
Luke, which is said to prove the historical untrustworthiness of
both (!) narratives ; and that asserted between the accounts of
Paul's visits to Jerusalem and his relations to the Twelve in
Acts and Galatians, which is said to prove the unhistorical
character of Acts. In the brief space at our disposal it ·is not
possible to disprove such wholesale charges in detail. It must
suffice, therefore, to point out the lines on which such a refutation proceeds. In the first instance the charge can be upheld
only by the expedient of assuming that silence as to an event
constitutes denial of that event, supported by criticisms which
tacitly deny a historian's right to give summary accounts of
transactions or choose his incidents according to his purpose in
writing. Any careful examination of the passages involved
will prove not only that they are not inconsistent, but rather

* That this was the custom in Asia Minor is evident from *Marturium
Polyc.*, c. 21, etc. Cf. also (in general) Pliny, *Nat. Hist.* ii. 77, and Plutarch,
Quaest Rom., lxxxiii.

† Cf. Townson's *Discourses*, Discourse 8: McClelland's *N. T.*, vol. i., p. 737
sq. ; Westcott on *John*, p. 282 ; Lee on *Inspiration*, p. 352 ; where this subject is fully discussed.

mutually supplementary accounts;* but also that they actually imply one another, and prove the truth of each other by a series of striking undesigned coincidences.† And when it is added that the choice of the material which each writer has made can in each incident be shown to have arisen directly out of the purpose of the writer, it may be seen what a load the assertion of disharmony must carry.

* The events recorded by Luke are—1. Annunciation to Zachariah; 2. Annunciation to Mary (in the sixth month thereafter); 3. Mary's visit to Elizabeth (extending to three months later); 4. Birth of John (after 3); 5. His circumcision (eight days after 4); 6. Journey of Joseph and Mary to Bethlehem (" in those days "); 7. Birth of Jesus (while at Bethlehem); 8. Annunciation to the shepherds (the same day); 9. Visit of the shepherds (hastening); 10. Circumcision of Jesus (eight days after); 11. Presentation (thirty-three days later); 12. Return to Nazareth (when all legal duties were performed). The events recorded by Matthew are—A. Mary is found with child (before she is taken to Joseph's house); B. Annunciation to Joseph; C. Mary is taken home by Joseph; D. Visit of the Magi (after Jesus' birth at Bethlehem); E. Flight into Egypt (after their departure); F. Slaughter of the innocents (when Herod had discovered that the wise men had gone); G. Death of Herod; H. Return from Egypt to Nazareth (after Herod's death). These events dovetail beautifully into one another, as follows: 1, 2, 3, 4, 5, A, B, C, 6, 7, 8, 9, 10, 11, D [12 (E, F, G, H)]. It is only necessary to assume that 12 includes E, F, G, and H compendiously, and all goes most smoothly. Other arrangements are also possible—e.g. the first half may be varied to 1, 2, A, B, C, 3, 4, 5, 6, or to 1, 2, A, 3, B, C, 4, 5, 6; and the second half to 9, 10, D, 11 [12—(E, F, G, H)], or even to 9, 10, D, E, F, G, half H, 11, half H —12. In the face of so many possible harmonizations it certainly cannot be asserted that harmony is impossible.

† Thus the account in the one of the annunciation to Joseph, and that in the other of that to Mary, which are often said to be irreconcilable with one another, actually prove each other's truth. Both assume exactly the same facts at their bases—viz. that Mary conceived a child supernaturally, and remained a virgin while becoming a mother. Moreover, if Luke's narrative be true, then something like what Matthew records must have happened; and if Matthew's be true, something like what Luke records must have happened. Two things needed explanation: why Mary was not crazed at finding herself so strangely with child, and how Joseph, being a just man, could have taken her, in that condition, to wife. Luke's narrative explains the first, but leaves the other unexplained; Matthew's explains the second, but leaves the first unexplained. It is admitted that there was no collusion here. How does it happen, then, that the two so imply one another? Again, Matthew does not mention where Jesus' parents lived before his birth, but only states that after that birth they intended to live in Bethlehem, and, after having been deterred from that, chose Nazareth. Now, why this strange choice? Luke, and Luke alone, supplies the reason: Nazareth was their old home. Still, again, that Luke calls Mary Joseph's " betrothed " in ii. 5 is not only remarkable, but totally inexplicable from Luke; we can only understand it when we revert to Matt. i. 25 and the preceding verses. These are but samples.

The asserted contradiction between Acts and Galatians is already crumbling of its own weight. Thus Keim, certainly no very "apologetic" critic, has shown very clearly that the passage in Galatians has suffered much eis-egesis in order to make out the disharmony,* and sober criticism will judge that even he has done inadequate justice to the subject. We cannot enter into details in so broad a question : it will be sufficient, however, to call attention to the fact that no disharmony can be made out unless—(1) Violence be done to the context in Galatians, where Paul professes to be giving an exhaustive account, *not* of his visits to Jerusalem, *but* of his opportunities to learn from the apostles. Any visit undertaken at such a time as to furnish no such opportunity (and Acts xii. was such) ought, therefore, to have been omitted. (2) Convenient forgetfulness be exercised of the fact that while the context shows that Paul uses "apostles" in the narrow sense in Gal. i. 19, yet this is not true of Acts ix. 27 ; but, as Luke's usage shows, the contrary may very well be true (Acts xiv. 4, 14). So that it is in no sense inconsistent for Paul to say that he saw but one apostle, and Luke that he saw several. (3) Misunderstanding be fallen into as to the nature of the "decree" of Acts xv. 20, and its binding force to churches not yet formed and not parties to the compromise. (4) Misrepresentation be ventured as to the testimony of Galatians as to Paul's relations to the Twelve, which Paul represents to have been most pleasant (Gal. ii. 3, 7-10), but which are made out to have been unpleasant through misinterpretation of phrases in Gal. ii. 2, 3, 4, 6, 9, etc. (5) Incredible pressure of the detailed language of both Galatians and Acts be indulged in. (6) And, finally, a tacit denial be made of the possibility of truth subsisting through differences in choice of incidents arising from the diverse points of view of the two writers. In other words, an unbiased comparison of the two accounts brings out forcibly the fact that there is no disharmony between them at all. Taking these examples as samples (and they are certainly fair samples), it is as clear as daylight that no single case has as yet been adduced where disharmony is a necessary conclusion. Therefore all charges from this side fall to the ground.

* In *Aus der Urchristenthum* (1878).

3. Another favourite charge against the exact truth of the
New Testament Scriptures is drawn from the use of the Old
Testament in the New, and especially the phenomena of its
quotation. Here also, however, most of the objections urged
prove nothing but a radical lack of clear thinking on the part
of those who bring them. For instance, Dr. Davidson argues[*]
that the verbal variation which the New Testament writers
allow themselves in quoting the Old Testament is conclusive
against verbal inspiration, for "the terms and phrases of the
Old Testament, if literally inspired, were the best that could
have been adopted," and therefore the New Testament writers
"should have adhered to the *ipsissima verba* of the Holy Spirit
(seeing they were the best) as closely as the genius of the
Hebrew and Greek languages allowed." Here, however, a
false view of inspiration is presupposed, and also a false view
of the nature and laws of quotation. Inspiration does not
suppose that the words and phrases written under its influence
are the best possible to express the truth, but only that they
are an adequate expression of the truth. Other words and
phrases might be equally adequate—might furnish a clearer,
more exact, and therefore better, expression, especially of those
truths which were subordinate or incidental for the original
purpose of the writing. Nor is quotation to be confounded with
translation. It does not, like it, profess to give as exact a representation of the original, in *all* its aspects and on *every* side,
as possible, but only to give a true account of its teaching in
one of its bearings. . There is thus always an element of application in quotation ; and it is therefore proper in quotation so
to alter the form of the original as to bring out clearly its bearing on the one subject in hand, thus throwing the stress on the
element in it for which it is cited. This would be improper in
a translation. The laws which ought to govern quotation seem,
indeed, to have been very inadequately investigated by those
who plead the New Testament methods of quotation against
inspiration. We can pause now only to insist—(1) That
quotation, being essentially different from translation, any

* *Hermeneutics*, p. 513.

amount of deviation from the original, *in form*, is thoroughly
allowable, so long as the sense of the original is adhered to;
provided only that the quoter is not professing to give the
exact form; (2) That any adaptation of the original to the
purpose in hand is allowable, so long as it proceeds by a true
exegesis, and thus does not falsify the original; (3) That any
neglect of the context of the original is allowable, so long as
the purpose for which the quotation is adduced does not imply
the context, and no falsification of sense is involved. In other
words, briefly, quotation appeals to the sense, not the wording,
of a previous document, and appeals to it for a definite and
specific end; any dealing with the original is therefore legitimate which does not falsify its sense in the particular aspect
needed for the purpose in hand.* The only question which is
relevant here, then, is, Do the New Testament writers so quote
the Old Testament as to falsify it?

Many writers who have pleaded the phenomena of the New
Testament against verbal inspiration yet answer this question
in the negative. Thus, Mr. Warington admits that there are
"no really inapposite quotations"—"the pertinency of the
quotations may be marred by their inaccurate citation, but
pertinent, notwithstanding, they always are. In a word, while
. . . the letter is often faulty, the spirit is always divinely
true." † This is simply to yield the only point in debate.
Others, however, of not such clearness of sight, do not scruple
to assert that the New Testament writers do deal so loosely
with the Old Testament as to fall into actual falsification, and
this mainly in two particulars: they quote passages in a sense
different from that which they bore in the Old Testament, and
they assign passages to wrong sources.

As an example of those who make the first charge we may

---

* Still, further: the amount of freedom with which a document is dealt
with will be greater in direct proportion to the thoroughness with which
it is understood. If a quoter feels doubtful as to his understanding of it,
he will copy it word for word; if he feels sure he understands it fully
and thoroughly, he will allow himself great freedom in his use of it; and
if he is the author of the original document, still more. If he is conscious
of having supernatural aid in understanding it, doubtless the amount of
freedom would be greatest of all.

† *Inspiration*, p. 107.

take Prof. Jowett, who is never weary of repeating it. * But when we ask for his proof, it is found to rest on four false assumptions, tacitly made: that difference in form means difference in sense, that typology is a dream, that application through a true exegesis is illegitimate, and that all adoption of language binds one to its original sense. Thus Prof. Jowett has difficulty in finding apposite examples, and those he does finally fix upon fail on examination.† Dr. Sanday, in his

---

* See *St. Paul's Epp.*, etc., vol. i., p. 353 *sq.*: London, 1855.

† The following are his examples: Rom. ii. 24, "where the words are taken from Isaiah, but the sense from Ezekiel." Possibly a true criticism; what is illegitimate in it? Note, however, that this is probably not a formal quotation, but an expression of Paul's own thought in Old Testament words, and hence the "as it is written" succeeds (not precedes) the quotation; this "as it is written" may therefore refer to Isaiah as quoted, or to Isaiah and Ezekiel, or to Ezekiel alone, now remembered by the apostle. (Compare Beet with Philippi Meyer *in loc.*) Rom. ix. 33, where only a composition of two passages takes place, which are rightly "harmonized," as Prof. J. admits, in Christ. 1 Cor. iii. 19, where the words are altered from the Psalm to suit the context indeed, but also in direct agreement with their context in the Psalm, so that no alteration in *sense* results. Rom. x. 11, which is called an "instance of the introduction of a word [πᾶς] on which the point of the argument turns," but which is simply a case of true exegesis and application to the matter in hand. The same passage, and without the πᾶς, had already been quoted in this context (ix. 33); Paul now requotes it, calling attention to the force of the unlimited ὁ πιστεύων by emphasizing its sense through an introduced πᾶς, and confirming his interpretation immediately by an additional Scripture (verse 13). Compare Luke xviii. 14, as given in Matt. xxiii. 14, as an example of like explanation. 1 Cor. xvi. 21, which is admitted to be a case "of addition rather than alteration," and any objection to which must rest on a tacit denial of typology, which even Meyer admits to be historically justifiable here. Rom. x. 6-9, presenting alterations which "we should hesitate to attribute to the apostle but for other examples, which we have already quoted, of similar changes," but which, even if considered as a quotation, is defensible enough; then how much more so when we note that it does not profess to be a quotation, and is probably nothing more than the expression of the apostle's thought in old and beloved words! 1 Cor. xv. 45, "a remarkable instance of discrepancy in both words and meaning from Gen. ii. 7." Quite true, and therefore neither in words nor meaning taken from Gen. 7. Prof. J. has simply neglected to note that the quotation extends only to ζῶσαν. (Cf. Meyer *in loc.*) Rom. x. 13, where the charge of change of meaning rests only on a misunderstanding of Mal. i 2, 3. Rom. iii. 10 *sq.*, "a cento of quotations transferred by the apostle [from their original narrow reference] to the world in general." As if Eccles. vii. 21, Ps. xiii. (xiv.) 12 were not already as universal as anybody could make them, and as if the choice of passages throughout was not admirably adapted to Paul's purpose, which was to prove that all men are sinners—yes, even the Jews. Rom. xii. 20, which requires no remark. And finally *six allegories*, which are immediately admitted not to be allegories in the only sense of the word which

excellent classification of New Testament quotations as to their form,* cites two passages only which can be plausibly asserted to be cases of mistaken ascription—viz. Mark i. 2 and Matt. xxvii. 9, 10. The first of these ought not to present any difficulty. The form of the sentence shows that the actual words of the citation are parenthetical in essence : Mark declares that John came preaching in accordance with a prophecy of Isaiah, and then inserts, parenthetically, the words referred to, adding also a parallel prophecy of Malachi. That he gives more evidence than he promised ought surely to be no objection ; it is enough that, having promised a prophecy from Isaiah, he does give it. This is strengthened by the fact that the prophecy quoted from Malachi is actually based on, and largely drawn out of, Isaiah, so that Isaiah is actually the ultimate source of both the prophecies given, and that from Malachi can be rightly looked upon as simply a further explanation of what is essentially Isaiah's. The quotation in Matt. xxvii. 9, 10, on the other hand, does present a difficulty, and is, indeed, in whatever aspect it be looked upon, a very puzzling case. It presents the extreme limit of paraphrase of the original, and it is exceedingly difficult to assign all its parts to their proper originals. It is plain, however, that Zech. xi. 13 was strongly colouring the writer's thoughts when he wrote it. Yet he ascribes it to Jeremiah. Here, it is said, is a clear case of erroneous ascription. This judgment, however, takes no account of the exceeding difficulty of ascribing the words actually quoted to Zechariah alone. There seem to be but three ways in which the passage can be plausibly understood, and no one of these implies an error on Matthew's part. We may either (1) understand the words as a very free paraphrase of Zech. xi. 13, and then appeal to the fact that in the Talmudic arrangement Jeremiah stood first in the " book of the prophets," so that Jeremiah here stands as general title for the whole book—with Lightfoot, Scrivener, Cook, Schaff-

would be to their disadvantage—*i.e.* in the sense of an interpretation which treated the literal sense of the words as unimportant, in which sense of the word no allegory occurs in the New Testament. These "allegories" are, some of them, simple illustrations, some *typical* interpretations.

* *Gospels in the Second Century*, pp. 16-25.

Riddle, etc.; or (2) take the reference in v. 9 as intended for Jer. xviii., xix.—apart from which passage, indeed, the quotation following cannot be understood—and suppose the quotation itself to be deflected to the words of Zechariah, so that the passage becomes analogous to Mark i. 2, and is meant to call attention to both Jeremiah and Zechariah—with (in general) Hengstenberg, Hofmann, Thrupp, Fairbairn, etc.; or (3) we may, with Lange, find the originals of the words in four passages in Genesis, Zechariah and Jeremiah, the key to the whole being Jer. xxxii. 6-8. Whichever of these views may be accepted is of no moment so far as the present question is concerned; each alike is consistent with the evangelist's truth, and therefore with his inspiration.

With these examples we must close. It is only necessary to add the caution that the passages dealt with are supposed by Mr. Jowett and Dr. Sanday to be the most striking and difficult ones that could be put to the apologist out of the two hundred and seventy-eight quotations which the New Testament makes from the Old. It is surely not presumptuous, then, to assert that Mr. Warington's wisdom is apparent, and that it is true that the New Testament quotations always preserve the sense of the Old Testament passages.

And with this, this paper must close. It has been possible, of course, to examine only samples of critical objection. But those that have been examined are samples, and have been selected wholly in the interests of the objection. These laid, therefore, and all are laid. The legitimate proofs of the doctrine, resting primarily on the claims of the sacred writers, having not been rebutted by valid objections, that doctrine stands doubly proved. Gnosis gives place to epignosis, faith to rational conviction, and we rest in the joyful and unshaken certainty that we possess a Bible written by the hands of men indeed, but also graven with the finger of God.

THE WESTMINSTER DOCTRINE OF INSPIRATION.

(With especial reference to some quotations by Dr. Briggs.)

BY PROF. BENJAMIN B. WARFIELD, D.D.,
PROFESSOR OF THEOLOGY IN PRINCETON SEMINARY.

[Reprinted by permission from the New York "Independent," December 5th, 1889.]

"CONTROVERSIALISTS in general," says the late Principal Cunningham, in one of his essays, "have shown an intense and irresistible desire to prove that their peculiar opinions were supported by the Fathers, or by the Reformers, or by the great divines of their own church; and have often exhibited a great want both of wisdom and candour in the efforts they have made to effect this object." We have earnestly sought to avoid this danger, and to assume a purely historical point of view in our study of the teaching of the British theologians of the Westminster age as to the extent and effect of inspiration. They are certainly entitled to have their opinions accurately represented; and we, on the other hand, would be unwilling to be understood as endorsing their whole teaching. Nevertheless, they appear to us very distinctly to teach both the verbal inspiration of the Scriptures and the inerrancy of the original autographs, and we have, therefore, felt it incumbent upon us to examine the evidence to the contrary which has been presented by Dr. C. A. Briggs in his recent book entitled ' Whither ? "

Dr. Briggs devotes two sections to the subject of the present paper (pp. 64-68 and 68-73). In the former he presents a catena of six quotations under the caption: " We shall give the opinions of a few Presbyterians of the seventeenth century on this subject, in order to show how far modern divines have departed from the Westminster doctrine of the Bible." It is perhaps not perfectly certain to what immediate antecedent the words " this subject " here refer. But in any event the catena of citations is meant to show that the Scriptures, in the estimation of the Westminster men, are not inspired in their " verbal expression." In the second section, two quotations are given to illustrate the statement that " the Westminster divines did not teach the inerrancy of the original autographs."

We take up the catena on verbal inspiration first ; and (on the principle of *ex pede Herculem*) we begin with the last quotation. It is from John Ball's Catechism and reads as follows :—

> " The testimonie of the Spirit doth not teach or assure us of the Letters, syllables, or severall words of holy Scripture, which are onely as a vessell, to carry and convey that heavenly light unto us, but it doth seale in our hearts the saving truth contained in those sacred writings into what language soever they be translated."

Now, on the assumption that the sole conclusive evidence that the Scriptures are the Word of God, is the Witness of the Holy Spirit in the heart, such a passage as this might seem to assert that only the matter of Scripture is inspired. But though this may be Dr. Briggs' point of view, it is not John Ball's. The very object of the passage quoted, is rather to guard against this overworking of the testimony of the Spirit : it is one of six rules which are given professedly " to prevent mistaking " in the use of this evidence. The immediately succeeding rule warns us that " the Spirit doth not lead them in whom it dwelleth, absolutely and at once into all truth, but into all truth necessary to salvation, and by degrees "; and one of the previous ones warns us not to forget that it is " private, not publique ; testifying only to him that is endued therewith." Ball's object, thus, is not to suggest that the Scriptures are not verbally inspired; *but to deny that this can be proved by "the testimonie of the Spirit."* By other forms of testimony, however (he teaches), it can be proved ; and resting upon them as giving a " certainty of the mind," he unhesitatingly teaches verbal inspiration. Let us hear his statement of it :—

E

" *Q.* What call you the Word of God ?

A. The holy Scripture immediately inspired, which is contained in the Books of the Old and New Testament.

Q. What is it to be immediately inspired ?

A. To be immediately inspired is to be as it were breathed, and to come from the Father by the Holy Ghost without all means.

Q. Were the Scriptures thus inspired ?

A. Thus the holy Scriptures in the Originals were inspired both for matter and words."

Examination of the other quotations, given in this catena, would lead us to similar results. In the first of them, for example, quoted from Lyford, the writer is not speaking of inspiration at all, but is arguing the widely different question whether the Word of God, that is, as he defines it (p. 46), "the mind and will of God," is so competently conveyed in translations that the unlearned may have in them a divine foundation for faith. But though he holds that "Divine Truth in English is as truly the Word of God, as the same Scripture delivered in the Originall Hebrew or Greek," he feels bound to add : "yet with this difference, that the same is perfectly, immediately and most absolutely in the Originall Hebrew and Greek, in other Translations, as the vessels wherein it is presented to us, and as far forth as they do agree with the Originalls." The difference between the originals and the translations arises from the fact that "the Translators were not assisted immediately by the Holy Ghost," while "such extraordinary assistance is needful to one that shall indite any part of Scripture" (p. 50). With all his tendency to defend the value of translations, therefore, he does not assimilate the inspiration of the originals to the divine element common to the two.

This enhancement of translations is carried perhaps a step higher by another of Dr. Briggs' witnesses, Richard Capel. The quotation which is made from him is somewhat spoiled in its effect on the reader by the omission of the italicizing which indicated the words that Capel was borrowing from his opponent. For Capel is here not calmly stating his own view, but controverting another's. He is inveighing against the carelessness of the welfare of human souls, which is shown by those

who dwell upon the uncertainties of copies and the fallibilities
of scribes and translators, as if the saving Word of God does
not persist through all these dangers. It is this mode of procedure which he says "lets in Atheisme like a flood"; the
passage quoted by Dr. Briggs being a positing of difficulties
which he at once sets himself "to help" by laying down a
series of contrary propositions. Accordingly he had said at an
earlier point (p. 38):—

   "I cannot but confesse that it sometimes makes my
heart ake, when I seriously consider what is said, *That
we cannot assure ourselves that the Hebrew in the Old
Testament and the Greek in the New, are the right Hebrew
and Greek, any further than our masters and tutors,
and the general consent of all the learned in the world
do so say, no one dissenting, ... all infallibility*
in matters of this nature having long since left the world.
. . . . And to the like purpose is that observation,
*That the two tables written immediately by Moses and
the Prophets, and the Greek copies immediately penned
by the Apostolical men are all lost, or not to be made use
of, except by a very few. And that we have none in
Hebrew or Greek, but what are transcribed. Now transcribers are ordinary men, subject to mistake, may faile,
having no erring spirit to hold their hands in writing.*
   "These be terrible blasts, and do little else when they
meet with a weak head and heart, but open the doore to
Atheisme and quite to fling off the bridle, which only can
hold them and us in the wayes of truth and piety: this
is to fill the conceits of men with evil thoughts against
the Purity of the Originalls: And if the Fountains run not
clear, *the Translation cannot be clean.*"

Capel's purpose, in a word, is not to depreciate the infallibility of the autographs, but to vindicate the general purity of
the transmission in copies and translations. The originals were
"the dictates of the Spirit," and their writers, being "induced
with the infallible Spirit," "might not erre" (cf. *Remains*, pp.
12, 38, 43, 55). His tendency was not to lower the autographs
towards the level of the translations, but to elevate the translations, so far as may be, towards the originals, *e.g.* claiming

for them a kind of secondary (providential) inspiration. Accordingly, although he would confess that the transmitters of Scripture had " no unerring spirit to hold their hands in writing," he yet asserted that God so assisted them " that for the main they should not erre," and " so held the hands and directed the pens of the Translators, that the translations might well be called the Word of God " (p. 31). No student of the history of doctrine need be told that the affinities of this view are with the highest. even the most mechanical theory of inspiration (cf. Ladd, *Doctrine of Sacred Scripture*, vol. ii., pp. 182 *sq.*).

Samuel Rutherford, the first writer whom Dr. Briggs quotes to prove that " The Westminster divines did not teach the inerrancy of the original autographs," is an even more extreme representative of the same type of thought that Capel stands for. If the reader will read the long passage quoted from him in " Whither ? " with an eye to the italics which mark the phraseology borrowed from John Goodwin whom Rutherford is here refuting, he will not fail to catch a hint of Rutherford's high doctrine. Rutherford here, in a word, is almost bitterly attacking Goodwin's assertions of the fallibility of the transmission of Scripture ; over against which he posits an " unerring and indeclinable providence " (p. 370) presiding over it. So far is he from suggesting that the autographs are not inerrant that he is almost ready to assert that all the copies and translations are inerrant too. He evidently feels himself to be making a great concession, and to be almost straining the truth, when he admits that there may be " errours of number, genealogies, etc., of writing in the Scripture as written " [*i.e.* in the manuscript form] " or printed." Though God has used means which, considered in themselves, are fallible in transmitting the Scriptures, yet he has not left the transmission to their fallibility, but has added an unerring providence, keeping them from slipping. He urges that Goodwin's argument " makes as much against Christ and his Apostles as against us," for they too had but copies of the Old Testament, the scribes and translators of which were " then no more than now, *immediately* inspired *Prophets*," and were consequently liable to errors : so that " if ye remove an unerring providence, who doubts but men might adde or subtract and so vitiate the fountaine sense? and omit points, change consonants, which in Hebrew and Greek both might quite alter the sense?" Yet both Christ and the apostles appeal to the Scriptures freely, with such phrases as "as David saith" and the like, staking their trustworthiness on the true transmission. Nor will he allow the argument that it is the inerrancy of the quoters, not of the text quoted, which is our safeguard in such cases. This, he says, presumes "that Christ and his apostles might and did finde errours and misprintings even in written" [i.e. manuscript] "Scripture, which might reduce the Church in after ages to an invincible ignorance in matters of faith, and yet they gave no notice to the Church thereof." To Rutherford, therefore, the whole Scriptures were spoken by the Holy Ghost (pp. 353-354), were all written by God (p. 373), are a more sure word than an immediate oracle from heaven (p. 193), and were written under an influence which secured them from error and mistake (pp. 366, 369, etc.).

It is an interesting indication of the universality of high views of inspiration that John Goodwin, Rutherford's adversary in this treatise, himself held them. So far as the points we are here interested in are concerned, indeed, the dispute was little more than a logomachy, since Rutherford and his friends were constrained to admit (though sometimes grudgingly) that the providential preservation of Scripture is not so perfect but that some errors have found their way into the copies, and that the translations are only in a derived sense the Word of God, and only so far forth as they truly represent the originals; while Goodwin was ready to allow that God's providence is active in preserving the manuscript transmission substantially pure, and that the truth of God is adequately conveyed in any good translation. In Goodwin's reply to his assailants it is made abundantly apparent that he too believed in the inerrancy of the autographs, his objection to calling copies and translations the Word of God, in every sense, turning just on this,—that no one extant copy or translation is errorlessly the Word of God (see *The Divine Authority of the Scriptures*, pp. 8, 9, 11, 12, 13).

But what about Richard Baxter? Dr. Briggs tells us that

he "was the leading Presbyterian of his time,' and that "he knew what he was about in his warning" which is quoted as Dr. Briggs' final proof that "the Westminster divines did not teach the inerrancy of the original autographs." But the passage that is quoted has again really nothing to do with the inerrancy of the autographs. It is only one of Baxter's frequently repeated statements of his sound apologetical position as to the relative value of different portions of Scripture and the relative importance of the sense and letter. It is partly on account of his firm grasp and clear expression and defence of this apologetical position, that we think of Baxter as one of the wisest and soundest writers on the subject of Scripture in his day. Despite the fact that he has been frequently misunderstood and misquoted, he did not doubt the verbal inspiration and autographic inerrancy of the Scriptures. It is one thing to refuse to make the verbal inspiration of the Scriptures the ground of all religion, and another thing to deny its reality. Baxter's chief works are accessible to all in Duncan's London edition of 1830, so that we may content ourselves here with the adduction of a passage or two in which he clearly asserts his belief in the inerrancy of the autographs of Scripture.

"All that the holy writers have recorded is true (and no falsehood in the Scripture, but what is from the error of scribes and translators)"—Vol. xv. p. 65.

"No error or contradiction is in it, but what is in some copies, by the failure of preservers, transcribers, printers and translators."—Vol. xxi. p. 542.

"If Scripture be so certainly true, then those passages in it that seem to men contradictory, must needs be true: for they do but seem so and are not so indeed."—Vol. xx. p. 27.

"These that affirm that it was but the doctrine of Christianity, that was sealed by the Holy Ghost, and in which they were infallible, but that their writings were in circumstantials and by-passages, and method and words, and other modal respects, imperfect and fallible, as other men's (in a less degree), though they heinously and dangerously err, yet do not destroy or hazard the Christian religion by it."—Vol. xx. p. 95.

" Though the Apostles were directed by the Holy Ghost in speaking and writing the doctrines of Christ, so that we know they performed their part without errors, yet the delivering down of this speech and writing to us, is a human work, to be performed with the assistance of ordinary providence."—Vol. xx. p. 115.

" All the credit of the Gospel and Christian religion doth not lie in the perfect freedom of the Scriptures from all error; but yet we doubt not to prove this their perfection against all the cavils of infidels, though we can prove the truth of religion without it."—Vol. xx. p. 118.

Let these serve as samples.

Probably no one man has a better right to be quoted as an exponent of the doctrine of the Westminster divines as a body, on this subject, than "the Patriarch of Dorchester," John White. He was chosen by them at the outset of their labours to serve as one of the two assessors, whose activity was expected to supplement the little public capacity of Twisse. His book— *Directions for the Profitable Reading of the Scriptures* (1647)— was introduced to the world by one of the leading Westminster divines, Dr. Thomas Goodwin, in a glowing eulogy. And Baxter (Vol. xxii. p. 335) names it among the works on the divine authority of the Scriptures which he especially recommends to the English reader. It is therefore a truly representative book. And we cannot do better than bring this paper to a close by adducing White's general statement as a fair representation of the prevalent view of his time. He founds his remarks on 2 Pet. i. 20, 21, and writes as follows:—

> " The Apostle . . . describes the kinde of assistance of the Holy Ghost in the delivery of the Scriptures, two ways, *First* by way of negation, that they were neither of private interpretation, nor came by the wil of man. *Secondly*, he describes the same assistance affirmatively, testifying that they spake as they were moved by the Holy Ghost.

" In the former of these, wherein he expresseth their manner of delivering the Scriptures by way of negation, the Apostle excludes the working of the naturall faculties of man's mind altogether : *First*, the understanding, when he denies that the Scripture is of any private interpretation, or rather of men's own explication, that is, it was not expressed by the understanding of man, or delivered according to man's judgment, or by his wisdome. So that not only the matter or substance of the truths revealed, but the very forms of expression were not of man's devising, as they are in Preaching, where the matter which men preach is not, or ought not to be the Minister's own, that preacheth, but is the word of truth, 2 Tim. 2, 15, but the tearms, phrases and expressions are his own. *Secondly*, he saith that it came not by the wil of man, who neither made his own choice of the matters to be handled, nor of the forms and manner of delivery. So that both the understanding and the wil of man, as farre as they were merely naturall, had nothing to doe in this holy work, save onely to understand, and approve that which was dictated by God himselfe, unto those that wrote it from his mouth, or the suggesting of his Spirit.

" Again, the work of the Holy Ghost in the delivery of the Scriptures is set down affirmatively, when the Pen-men of those sacred writings are described to speak as they were moved by the Holy Ghost, a phrase which must be warily understood. For we may not conceive that they were moved in writing these Scriptures, as the pen is moved by the hand that guides it, without understanding what they did : For they not only understood, but willingly consented to what they wrote, and were not like those that pronounced the Devil's oracles, rapt and carried out of themselves by a kinde of extasie, wherein the Devill made use of their tongues and mouths to pronounce that which themselves understood not. But the Apostle's meaning is, that the Spirit of God moved them in this work of writing the Scriptures, not according to nature but above nature shining into their understandings clearly and fully by a heavenly and supernatural light, and carrying and moving their wils thereby with a delight and holy enhancing of that truth revealed, and with a like desire to publish and make known the secrets and counsels of God, revealed unto them, unto the Church.

" Yea beyond all this, the Holy Ghost not only suggested unto them the substance of that doctrine which they were to deliver and leave upon record unto the Church (for so far he usually assists faithful ministers in dispensing of the Word in the course of their Gospel ministry), but besides, has supplied unto them the very phrases, method and whole order of those things that are written in the Scriptures, whereas he leaves ministers in preaching the Word to the choice of their own phrases and expressions, wherein, as also in some particulars which they deliver, they may be mistaken, although in the main fundamentals which they lay before their hearers, and in the general course of the work of their ministry they do not grossly erre. Thus then the Holy Ghost, not only assisted holy men in penning the Scriptures, but in a sort took the work out of their hands, making use of nothing in the men, but of their understandings to receive, and comprehend, their wils to consent unto, and their hands to write down that which they delivered. When we say that the Holy Ghost framed the very phrase and style wherein the Scriptures were written, we mean not that he altered the phrase and manner of speaking, wherewith custome and education had acquainted those that wrote the Scriptures, but rather speaks his own words, as it were in the sounds of their voice, or chooseth out of their words and phrases such as were fit for his own purpose. Thus upon instruments, men play what lesson they please, but the instrument renders the sound of it more harsh or pleasant according to the nature of itself. Thus amongst the Pen-men of Scriptures, we finde that some write in a rude and more unpolished style, as *Amos;* some in a ·more elegant phrase, as *Isay.* Some discover art and learning in their

74

writings, as S. *Paul*; others write in a more vulgar way,
as S. *James*. And yet with all, the Spirit of God drew
their natural style to a higher pitch, in divine expressions, fitted to the subject on hand" (Pp. 59-62).

It is almost pathetic to observe White's efforts to mitigate
the effects of his mechanical conception of the mode of inspiration, in the matter of the style of the authors. Others made
similar efforts and sometimes with more success. But the
time had not yet come when the true synergism of inspiration,
by which we may see that every word of Scripture is truly
divine and yet every word is as truly human, had become the
common property of all. In this, too, therefore, White is a fair
exponent of his day, and reminds us anew that so far from
denying verbal inspiration and the inerrancy of Scripture, the
tendency to error of the times was in the opposite direction;
and in the strenuousness of its assertion of the fact of an
inspiration which extended to the expression and secured
infallibility, it was ever in danger of conceiving its mode in
a mechanical way. That this was the ruling attitude of the
middle of the seventeenth century among the Continental
theologians, whether Reformed or Lutheran, everybody knows.
It is clear, from what we have seen, that the English Puritans
and Scotch Presbyterians were not an isolated body cut off
from the currents of thought of their day; but were in harmony
with the best theologizing and highest conceptions of their
Continental brethren.

Princeton, N. J.

APPENDIX.

In *The Presbyterian and Reformed Review* for April (New York) the following appears as a critique on the recently-issued pamphlets of Dr. Blaikie, Dr. Watts, and Mr. Howie on the Dods and Bruce cases:—" Quite a little literature on inspiration bids fair to grow up in Scotland out of the manifesto issued by those who were dissatisfied by the disposition made of the cases of Drs. Dods and Bruce at the last Free Church Assembly. It is ominous of much that men of undoubted reverence for the Bible like Dr. Blaikie eagerly take up the cudgels for a loose doctrine of inspiration—how loose Dr. Blaikie does not seem to understand himself, as he rings the changes on 'infallibly' and 'verbally' correct on the one hand and 'substantially accurate' on the other, and yet seeks to disprove the former by adducing substantial and 'material' errors (p. 8); and arrays the phenomena of Scripture against its assertions, as if these assertions were not just the chief phenomenon of importance in the case and as if the next most outstanding phenomenon was not the use of the Old Testament by the writers of the New, the significance of which even his co-Free-Churchman, Mr. Stuart, in his *Principles of Christianity*, might have taught him. Dr. Blaikie is mistaken in supposing that the loose view that he represents is inductively established, while *a priori* reasoning is the support of those who hold to plenary inspiration ; the difference in procedure is precisely as it is stated by Dr. Watts, in his crushing reply : ' While the principle of your theory is a mere inference from apparent discrepancies not yet explained, the principle of the theory you oppose is the formally expressed utterance of prophets and apostles and of Christ Himself ' (p. 30). The whole issue really turns on the ' methodology :' shall we begin with the Scripture doctrine of inspiration and then consider whether this doctrine is supported or negatived by the phenomena, or shall we begin with the 'difficulties' of Scripture and then seek to minimize the Scripture doctrine to fit our ability or inability to explain the 'difficulties.' If the former path is taken we shall certainly end in a doctrine of 'verbal,' or, as it is less ambiguously called, 'plenary' inspiration; for on any fair exegesis this is indubitably the doctrine of the Bible writers and none of the phenomena negative it. If the latter is taken, we may land in the fogs. All this and more is pointed out, however, by Dr. Watts and Mr. Howie in their rejoinders. We can take time to speak here only of the singularly temperate strength and well guarded language of Mr. Howie's reply, badly requited as it is by Dr. Blaikie's angry and unjust postcript."

Referring to " that recent attempt to hide an essentially rationalistic attitude towards Holy Scripture under the name of the *testimonium Spiritus sancti*, of which Dr. Briggs is the best known American exponent," *The Presbyterian and Reformed Review* further says: " The essential difference between this destructive modern theory and the Protestant doctrine of the *testimonium Spiritus sancti*, is that the latter conceives of the Spirit as acting by quickening our apprehension of the strength of the various evidences, thus producing a conviction which is rational in its form and divine in its strength and source ; while the modern theory begins by discrediting the evidences and is thus shut up to conceiving of the testimony of the Spirit either as a special revelation or a blind conviction, framed apart from or prior to or even against the evidences. This brings this definition of the testimony of the Spirit into analogy with that definition of faith which makes it the power to believe to be true what we clearly see to be false. Thus it separates science and faith and must ultimately reduce one or the other to an 'innocuous desuetude.' "

In keeping with what is stated by Dr. Warfield in the above critique about "methodology" I add the following extract from the writings of the late Principal Cunningham :—" Dr. Chalmers' doctrine of inspiration is just that which has been the general doctrine of the universal Church in all ages—that, namely, of the imfallibility of the sacred record without including any definite deliverance upon the more minute and perplexing questions that have been raised about the nature and the mode of inspiration ; and to call this doctrine 'crude and unintelligible' is a simple absurdity, or rather it is mere unmeaning abuse. As to its being 'inadmissible,' this of course depends upon the evidence which can be adduced for and against it, and on the consideration of that we cannot at present enter. We believe it can be, and has often been, proved, that the Scriptures virtually assert their own inspiration and infallibility, and that we may reasonably receive this upon their testimony without being justly chargeable with the fallacy of reasoning in a circle; and, moreover, that the objections adduced against this doctrine are quite insufficient to neutralize the direct positive evidence on which it rests. Some of the objections, no doubt, are possessed of considerable plausibility, though not as we think can be shown, of any real weight. Indeed we have always been disposed to regard the subject of the evidence of inspiration as affording a good test of the soundness of men's understandings, as fitted, speaking generally, to mark off men into two classes, the higher class consisting of those who take a firm grasp of the direct, proper, primary evidence, who keep objections and difficulties in their proper place as objections and difficulties, and estimate them in their relation to the evidence at their true worth and value; and the lower class, consisting of those who are more easily perplexed and upset by objections and difficulties, and who are less competent to take a sound, comprehensive, and discriminating view of the evidence as a whole."

SCOTLAND AND THE BIBLE.

WE noticed some time ago the signs of approaching battle in the Free Church of Scotland. These begin to thicken. We had first of all a " Statement by minsters and other office bearers," taking the gravest exception to the recent decisions of the General Assembly in regard to Drs. Dods and Bruce. The very issue of that document was significant. Scotchmen are not much given to vapouring; and to those, who know the deep loyalty of Free Churchmen to the Decisions of their Church Courts, the publication of the Statement must have seemed like the premonitory crack that heralds the avalanche. The intervention of Professor Blaikie has not allayed the apprehensions of one party nor crushed the rising hopes of the other. It has merely given occasion to Mr. Howie to carry, in his masterly reply, the war into the enemy's camp.

One cannot but marvel why the Courts of the Free Church should be made the battle-field of this great controversy. What a fate for the Church of Chalmers and of Guthrie, of Candlish and of Cunningham, of the Bonars and, we may add, of M'Cheyne, who would have found in it a home in which his soul would have delighted! It is quite possible that, in a way, the fact may find an explanation. The students of the Free Church may have sought the schools of Germany in larger numbers than those of other denominations. But it would still have to be explained why they should have brought home a taint with them which others found it impossible to carry. We must look beyond these things to the Divine purpose. God has not forsaken a Church which in the past has served Him so well, and which still loves Him fervently. No! He has further work for it to do, and He must prepare it for service. He will lead it away from dependence upon the word of man's wisdom, and kindle once more the fires of evangelical ardour. He will break the yoke of this Christian Rabbinism, and stay the ossification which is changing Christ-like zeal and freedom into dull formality and bloodless respectability.

That, we believe, is one purpose of this "day of rebuke"; and we are no less convinced that there is another. The battle with rationalism must be joined somewhere; and the Divine wisdom has suffered unbelief to seize the high places of a Church that is zealous for the truth, that has well-defined beliefs, and a perfectly defensible position. The Free Church is not alone in this terrible experience. There are other churches in a similar position; but, with the exception of a groan here and there, there is no sign that the change is deplored or even marked. So far as they are concerned, the dry rot of rationalism would be permitted to eat into the fabric of faith till the whole should fall in shapeless ruin. It may be true, as they sometimes say, that they could do little, were they even to try. But it is painfully evident that they have no mind to try. The Free Church, however, is made of sterner stuff. Their loyalty to God is still a fact, and, we might almost add, a passion. Descendants of men who sacrificed good name and fortune, and freedom and life for the truth which God has committed to us, they are not likely to be intimidated by a little temporary unpopularity, or to be annihilated by the sneers of so-called learning. There is no church in the land where men can be found with clearer and deeper conviction, and with more absolute tidelity. Place this fact by the side of the other of which we have spoken—that the Free Church Creed is a living thing, and not a shibboleth, and that the position of orthodoxy is clearly defined, and easily defensible—and you can understand why this should be the chosen battle-field of the time. It will be the Waterloo of rationalism. The French spirit has overpowered the German host, but in vain will it pour its rain of fire upon these serried ranks. It will spend its strength and meet its doom, and haply, as of old, the scattered Germans may rally again and join in the pursuit, and chase the discredited thing back to its native home—the bosom of the men who are too great and too wise to need God.

We have frequently said that Mr. Bradlaugh will now have abundant leisure to attend to his Parliamentary duties. The same view is expounded in a recent issue of the *Edinburgh Evening News*. "The *National Reformer* for years," it says, " combated vigorously the idea of infallibility, and made capital out of the mistakes and immoralities of the Bible. Mr. Bradlaugh now finds his views so ably aired in the Church of England and the Free Church of Scotland, that his occupation is gone." That this is really the case is apparent, even from Professor Blaikie's letter. He occasionally writes as if the question were one as to *theories* of inspiration, rather than as to the *product* of inspiration—as to how the Bible came into existence, and not as to what the Bible is. But the bulk of his pamphlet shows clearly that the quarrel of himself and his party is not with theories of inspiration, but with the estimation in which the Bible is ordinarily held. This Free Church Professor teaches his students, and contends before the British public, that there are " verbal and substantial discrepancies" in the Scripture ; that is, that in different accounts of the same incident, there are not only variations in statement, but also distinct and undeniable contradictions, so that there is falsehood in one account, if not in all. Has Mr. Bradlaugh ever said anything worse than that ? and, if he could make such words good, would he require to do more to leave us, like himself, without hope and without God in the world ? That we are not misrepresenting the Professor will be only too plain from the following statements which meet us on page after page of his pamphlet. Addressing Dr. Bonar, he says, " You say it cannot be conceived that there was any inaccuracy in the original Scriptures. I appeal to the facts of the case in opposition to your view." He has thrown away the notion that the Bible as originally given was "absolutely free from error," because it involves him in "inextricable difficulties." Here is a description of Scripture which, if it lack in elegance, clearly enough foreshadows the proposed new Free Church reconstruction of the Old Testament : " bits of history and biography, poetry and song, didactic teaching and symbolic vision, had all been shot, as it were, into one capacious reservoir." He contends that the words of the Confession of Faith, " God, the Author of Holy Scripture," must not be pressed. It is " unwarrantable " to claim " that God is an author to precisely the same effect as man." If these words mean anything, they mean that the Bible is not a communication from God in as real a sense as a " Letter to the Rev. A. Bonar, D.D.," is a communication from Dr. Blaikie. We are also informed that it is a delicate task " to reconcile Old Testament morality in some points with the inspiration of Scripture." If this is true, the case must be very bad indeed ; for, with Dr. Blaikie, the term " Inspiration " seems elastic enough to cover a great deal.

Such are the views which this Professor of the Free Church now confesses he has been communicating to his students for the last 12 or 15 years. He also aired them, he says, before a clerical society. He does not say that he ever preached them to the people. But to the people of Scotland this cause must now go. If they profess themselves as willing to surrender the Scripture as Dr. Blaikie and his colleagues we shall be surprised. But even if they did, the duty of faithful men would be only rendered the more imperative. Those to whom, in the Free Church, the cause of truth is committed, would not even then be ashamed of the testimony of the Lord and of His apostles. Let them be of good courage. He who brought them out of Egypt will also deliver from the Philistine.—" *The King's Own,*" Feb., 1891.

LETTERS TO PROFESSOR DRUMMOND.

I.

4 BRUCE ROAD, POLLOKSHIELDS,
17th December, 1890.

DEAR PROFESSOR DRUMMOND,

Herewith I send copy of the Second Edition of my Reply
to Dr. Blaikie. At pages 77, 8, you will see references to your correspondence with me. As you have not yet corrected the *Herald's*
report of your Inaugural Address, and as I have ascertained that your
MSS. were in the hands of the reporter of that journal, I do not feel at
liberty at present to go beyond what I there state. I am more than
ever persuaded that you will not do justice to yourself, to the Church
of which you are a professor, or to the cause of Foreign Missions and
of Divine truth, unless you either correct that report or publish your
address as delivered. I may add that the unfavourable impression at
first produced on my mind by reading that address as given in the
Herald, instead of being altered, has rather been confirmed by your
Christmas booklet, *Pax Vobiscum.* While I appreciate its fine
writing, I am saddened by its lamentably defective and misleading
views of Divine truth. Although your theme specially demanded
such references, I am grieved to find that, from beginning to end,
there does not appear to be a single express reference to the guilt of
sin as a cause of unrest, to the need of pardon, to the imputation of
Christ's righteousness, to the atonement of Christ, to the work of the
Holy Spirit in regeneration, or to His operations in the hearts of
believers. If you had prayerfully studied in its connection the " Pax
Vobiscum " spoken by the risen Lord to His disciples, I can scarcely
conceive it possible that you would have so missed a great opportunity of helping those who are " seeking rest and finding none " by
giving, as you do, such an inadequate view of the nature and grounds
of a sinner's peace, and by perverting so thoroughly the grand words
of Jesus Christ—" I will give you rest."

Any heathen moralist might have written your booklet. The
homage you give to Christ seems a mere mockery, inasmuch as you
represent Him as doing nothing more, in the way of giving peace and
rest, than might have been done by Aristotle, Socrates, or Plato.

F

Perhaps you will again tell me that in all this I misunderstand and misrepresent your meaning, and that, although the above doctrines are not expressed, they are implied, and form part of your creed.

If you can say so much, it will be to me, as a brother presbyter, a great relief. But even in that case my answer must be that you have woefully failed in your duty as a Christian teacher, when, addressing so many readers on a subject plainly requiring it, you make no express reference to these vitally important truths.

You must surely feel that there must be something radically wrong in your way of putting matters when even the *British Weekly* (generally characterized by a friendly tone towards the school to which you belong) has felt it to be incumbent to remonstrate with you as to the teaching of this, your latest, production. I write in sorrow, but in faithfulness, and in the hope that I shall have from you some satisfactory explanation in regard to the points of which your co-presbyters have reason to complain. As this is a matter of public importance, affects the Church as a whole, and involves the vindication of Divine truth, I may feel it to be my duty either to publish this letter, or to bring the matter before the Presbytery. In these circumstances, I hope you may consent to the publication of any reply you may see fit to send.—With kind regards, I am, yours very truly,

ROBERT HOWIE.

II.

4 BRUCE ROAD, POLLOKSHIELDS,
25th December, 1890.

DEAR PROFESSOR DRUMMOND,

Thanks for yours of the 22nd instant. As mine of the 17th instant related to your published utterances, I am surprised that instead of consenting to the publication of your reply you have again marked it " private." You cannot now say, as you did before, that you adopt this course, because you will thus " least expose " me " to shame," for you know that I asked you to consent to the publication of your reply. You moreover seem strangely forgetful of the fact that others beside myself need to be satisfied about your published views. You say you are at a loss to understand why in the second edition of my pamphlet I have not withdrawn "the Appendix itself," which you repudiated in yours of the 28th ultimo. If I had done so, your repudiation (which I publish) would have been meaningless. Its references would not have been understood by my readers. But that is not all. In that repudiation you charge me with putting words into your mouth which you never spoke. As all the words I attribute to you in the Appendix were taken from the *Herald's* report of your Inaugural Address, I could not show the utter groundlessness of your charge as made against myself, except by allowing the Appendix to stand in its original form so that readers might compare its quotations with the report of the *Herald*. And this I was the more entitled to do, not only because I have also published your repudiation, but also because, although specially asked to do so, you have not yet corrected the *Herald's* report. If you either correct it, or tell me in what respect it is incorrect, I will be able to say to what extent my comments on your address should be modified, but otherwise, I have no alternative but to adhere to them. You say :— "The *Herald* Reporter did *not* get my MSS. He got four or five pages (out of some 30) near the middle as he wished specially to have this passage." I assume that to that extent the report quoted is correct. If in other respects it is incorrect, you ought surely long ere this, and for the sake of every interest concerned, to have made the necessary correction. You say further :—" As to *Pax Vobiscum*, to quote your own letter, ' you will again tell me that in all this I misunderstand your etc.' This is precisely the state of the case. It is mere affectation to say that it is not obvious all through this address that it is spoken to *Christians*, and that it is on the subject of ' *Christian experiences.*' Apart from that, you cannot surely have read the words (page 50) ' were Rest my subject, there are other things I should wish to say about it, *and other kinds of Rest of* which I should like to speak. *But that is not my subject.* My subject is etc.' "

I am most anxious not to misunderstand you. Will you therefore kindly say whether your words (" This is precisely the state of the case ") apply to the whole sentence in my letter, or only to the part quoted by you ? The sentence in full is as follows :—" Perhaps you will again tell me that in all this I misunderstand and misrepresent your meaning, and that, although the above doctrines are not expressed, they are implied, an ' form part of your creed."

As you include " etc." in the marks of quotation you use, the fair
interpretation seems to be that your affirmation (" This is precisely
the state of the case ") is intended by you to apply to the whole sentence. But as your language is also capable of another meaning, and
may be intended to apply only to the words you actually quote, I hope
you will not regard me as too exacting when, with the view of preventing further misunderstanding, I ask you specially whether the doctrines
referred to in mine of the 17th instant (viz., " the guilt of sin as
a cause of unrest," " the need of pardon," " the imputation of
Christ's righteousness," " the atonement of Christ," " the work
of the Holy Spirit in regeneration," and " His operations in the
hearts of believers ") are intended to be " implied " in your booklet
though not expressed, and whether they " form part of your creed."
I put these questions the rather because I do not regard what you say
about your address being spoken to " *Christians*," and " on the subject
of *Christian experiences*," as any justification whatever of the omission
by you of express reference to these important doctrines when treating of Christian rest or peace. I know of no genuine " Christian
experience " of rest or peace which does not involve these doctrines,
and hence the prominence given to them in Apostolic epistles which
were addressed to " Christians," and which treat of " Christian experiences." This I say, apart from the fact that the great promise of
Christ (" I will give you rest ") of which you treat is one addressed
not to Christians but to the Christless, as a promise to be realized
when they come to Him. The manner in which you seek to explain
away that precious promise appears to me to manifest either strange
confusion of thought, or sadly defective theology.

Being most unwilling to find you holding erroneous views, I will
gladly accept any explanation of your real meaning with which you
may favour me. But you need not wonder that your booklet has
given grave offence to many of your brethren, containing, as it does,
such statements as the following :—" Rest, apparently, was a favour
to be bestowed ; men had but to come to Him ; He would give it to
every applicant. But the next sentence takes that all back. . . .
When Christ said He would give men rest, He meant simply that
He would put them in the way of it. By no act of conveyance would,
or could, He make over His own rest to them. He could give His
receipt for it. That was all. But He would not make it for them; for
one thing, it was not in His plan to make it for them ; for another
thing, men were not so planned that it could be made for them ; and

for yet another thing, it was a thousand times better that they should make it for themselves. . . . Wounded vanity, then, disappointed hopes, unsatisfied selfishness—these are the old, vulgar, universal sources of man's unrest. . . . The ceaseless chagrin of a self-centred life can be removed at once by learning Meekness, and Lowliness of heart. . . . Christ's invitation to the weary and heavy-laden is a call to begin life over again upon a new principle—upon His own principle. 'Watch My way of doing things,' He says. 'Follow Me. Take life as I take it. Be meek and lowly, and you will find rest.'"

If, notwithstanding these and similar statements in your booklet, which seem to be capable of only one interpretation, you also hold that the sense of guilt is the leading cause of the unrest of men ; that (to use the words of the *British Weekly*) " the Christian pain is the agony of a wounded conscience, the desire to obtain release from the days of old, the longing for reconciliation with God "; that " there are other sorrows that appeal not vainly to the heart of Christ : agonies of pain and loss and care "; that " the sufferers creep to His side for shelter, and find it in the cleft of the wound "; that " they are hidden in His Peace as in a fortress-home "; that Christ gives the Holy Ghost, one of whose fruits is " peace "; if you hold all this, and had it in your view, when (at p. 50) you refer to " other things" you "should wish to say about it" [Rest], and to " other kinds of Rest of which " you "should like to speak," I will be truly glad if our correspondence shall elicit from you such an explanation, and shall furnish you with an opportunity of so far remedying the obvious defects of your booklet.

But if this is to be accomplished, I humbly submit that as so many others have attached to it the same meaning as I have done, you should either consent to the publication of our correspondence, or, of your own accord, publish such a statement as will remove existing misconceptions.

Meanwhile, reserving, as before, my right to publish my side of the correspondence, and with kind regards,—I am, yours very truly,

ROBERT HOWIE.

III.

4 BRUCE ROAD, POLLOKSHIELDS,
5th January, 1891.

DEAR PROFESSSOR DRUMMOND,

I am in receipt of yours of the 31st ultimo. Although I put plain questions, so as to obtain answers which might prevent misunderstanding on my part as to your views, I regret that, of the several doctrines which I specified, you refer only to that of "sin," substituting, however, the word "sense" for "guilt," when referring to it. I regret further that you make no reference whatever to the objectionable passages I quoted from your booklet. Notwithstanding my desire to "think no evil" our correspondence has thus only confirmed the unfavourable impression I had formed as to your views on the vital points in question. It still remains with me to consider what may be my duty as your co-presbyter. Having just heard from one of your students that you mean forthwith to publish your Inaugural Address, I shall delay taking action in the hope that this information may prove to be correct, and that the address when published in full may tend to modify the unfavourable impression which the *Herald* report of it has produced, and which has been confirmed by *Pax Vobiscum* and by your letters to myself. With the compliments of the season and kind regards.—I am, yours very truly,

ROBERT HOWIE.

POSTSCRIPT.

I HAVE just seen the pamphlet of Rev. William Grant, M.A., on "The Defence of Scripture on Scientific Lines with reference to the Manifesto on the Dods and Bruce Cases." I would have taken no notice of it, but for the fact that its author misrepresents (doubtless unintentionally) the "method of defence" of Scripture adopted by those who are responsible for the Manifesto. He tries to make it appear—although he gives no proof whatever of his averments—that they adopt what he describes as the "traditional" or "scholastic" method, which "starts with the product of inspiration, the infallible record, as its basis, or premiss," as against the "scientific" method which "starts with the product of revelation, the infallible substance, or truth of Scripture, as its basis."

The pamphlet is written in such a style that it is somewhat difficult to know, even after all the explanations of its author, what precisely is intended by the contrast here drawn. If, however, Mr. Grant means to assert that in defending Scripture those responsible for the Manifesto begin by assuming the infallibility of the record as the product of inspiration, and thence deduce the reality, infallibility, and Divine authority of the revelation, I have no hesitation in saying that he misrepresents the " method of defence " of Scripture adopted by his brethren. The order we follow in dealing with Sceptics is well stated by Drs. Hodge and Warfield under the heading of " Presuppositions " (p. 29). We do not begin with the evidence which immediately establishes inspiration, far less do we assume the infallibility of the record, but we first establish theism, then the historical credibility of the Scriptures, and then the Divine origin of Christianity, and thus the infallibility and authority of the revelation of God's will which the Scriptures contain. Having done all this, we are in a position to present, in convincing form, the evidence in favour of the inspiration and consequent infallibility of the record, based on the statements of Biblical writers, and of Christ and His Apostles. " Reasoning then from this infallible foundation " (to use the words of Mr. Grant) " there follows from infallible truth by logical deduction, infallible objective statements, and also infallible text. . . . From the express declarations of Scripture as to the inspiration of the ' written Word,' ' the Scriptures,' and from the example of Christ and His Apostles making an argument depend upon a particular form of a word, there is evidence of a verbal inspiration, or of an inspiration of the written Word itself, to secure that the moral and spiritual truth of Scripture is infallibly transmitted. If this were not so, inspiration as distinct from revelation, would be a mere name without effect."

www.ingramcontent.com/pod-product-compliance
Lightning Source LLC
Chambersburg PA
CBHW031452270326
41930CB00007B/957

* 9 7 8 3 7 4 3 3 7 3 5 7 0 *